Great Yachts
and their
Designers

Great Yachts
and their
Designers

Jonathan Eastland

FOREWORD BY ROBERT E. DERECKTOR

Rizzoli
New York

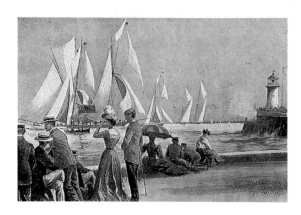

Page 1: *The Champagne Mumm Admiral's Cup fleet in action in the Solent.* Page 2: *The restored J class yacht Velsheda, designed by Charles E. Nicholson.* Left: *Members of the Royal Temple Yacht Club at Ramsgate watching the races on July 14, 1900. Watercolor sketch by Charles de Lacy.*

Acknowledgments
This book could not have been completed without the help of many dedicated people. In particular, my thanks go to Ray Eastland, Andy Rose, and Caroline Beaumont for their help with researching historical material; to Adrian Morgan and Jim McCaig for their work on the story of *Britannia*. My thanks also to my publisher, Cindy Parzych, for patience beyond the call, and to Kate Beckman for her help in researching many of the illustrations.

First published in the United States of America in 1987 by
RIZZOLI INTERNATIONAL PUBLICATIONS, INC.
597 Fifth Avenue, New York, NY 10017

Library of Congress Cataloging-in-Publication Data

Eastland, Jonathan.
  Great yachts and their designers.

  Includes index.
  1. Yachts and yachting. 2. Yachts and yachting—Design and construction. 3. Yacht designers.
  I. Title.

VM331.E27   1987   623.8'223   87-45388
ISBN 0-8478-0828-9
Created and produced by Cynthia Parzych Publishing, Inc.
Editor: Jay Hyams
Designer: Adrian Taylor
Photo researcher: Kate Beckman
Composition by Cosmos Communications, Inc., New York
Separations by Laser Graphics, Hong Kong
Printed and bound by Tien Wah Press, Singapore

Contents

For Alwyn John Foulkes, mate and mentor
through so many voyages of adventure

Opposite: Sayula, *Mexican
millionaire Ramon Carlin's
ketch-rigged Swan 65, was
the overall handicap winner
of the first Whitbread Round-
the-World Race in 1974.*
Above: Maurice Laing's
Bathsheba *during the stormy
start of the 1985 Fastnet
Race.* Right: Warren Luhrs
designed Thursday's Child,
*a revolutionary ULDB with
water ballasting, with
Paul Lindenburg and Lars
Bergstrom and raced it
in the 1984 OSTAR.*

Foreword

If one wants to design boats, one should look at fish, or look at the way water flows; watch the movement. With boat design, inspiration should come from the water, from the element itself. There's a strong tendency in boat design today to copy what other people have done, what other people have made work—copy it and then put your own fingerprint on it. I don't like that. Rather than imitate what someone else has done, I like to develop a shape that fits a certain wind and sea condition yet still gives an owner what he should have. I enjoy sailing on the sea a lot, and I like to watch the effects the sea and wind have on a given piece of equipment. I observe and then try to come to a new, independent solution.

I was thirteen when I designed and built my first boat, a 26-foot cutter. I built it because that was the only way I was going to get a boat. I sailed it in Long Island Sound and toward and around Nova Scotia.

The boats you read about and hear about most are racing boats. There's a reason for that: most of the development and forward thinking in the field goes into racing boats. That doesn't necessarily make them the best all-around boats. Racing boats are influenced by a rule and a desire to win under that rule that may make them an unhealthy, or unsound, type.

The San Diego Yacht Club's
12M America's Cup challenger
Stars & Stripes, *skippered by*
Dennis Conner, successfully
retrieved the cup for America
off Fremantle in 1987.

Technology goes in waves: boats first are made light for speed, then they are made too light; many fail. Reaction to that makes them stronger and heavier again. I prefer to observe on my own—I like to watch a design and try it out and make it right. I don't like to be unduly influenced by rules, which almost inevitably provide unhealthy types of boats. The elements—wind and water—should be allowed to determine design. They stimulate the most sensible answers to design.

Designs change; materials change. Today we're getting more and more into synthetics and so-called composites. Most metals are good for structure; titanium is excellent; composites are also good when they're used the right way. I myself don't like to handle epoxy resins, and from a long-life point of view perhaps I don't like them. All these materials have a use and a place, and soon they'll show up in airplane design and construction.

There will always be a market for boats. The biggest question is, do you give the buyer what he believes he wants, or do you give him what he ought to have? In the end, you should give him what he ought to have for his particular use.

This book presents a history of various yacht designers. It's an interesting story, and although it's probably been told many times before, I think this is the first book to put it all together in the same volume. Anyone who is deeply interested in this field will have encountered much of this information in other places. And one can get tired of words. After reading and looking at pictures, you want to get out and use, feel, and see the real thing in action.

ROBERT E. DERECKTOR
Coddington Cove, Middletown, R.I.

Preface

There can be few people who own boats or desire to own them for purely pleasurable reasons who do not choose them—after all practical considerations are made—on a subjective basis. "A thing of beauty is a joy forever."

In this context, it matters not whether a yacht is fast or faster than another, a winner of one cup or winner of a thousand. As I know from experience of sailing with and working alongside sailors, recognition of elegant shape and form in any vessel is frequently manifested in long and varied discussion. There are the inevitable comparisons, the arm-long lists of boat names long forgotten, the performance statistics of certain ocean greyhounds in weather conditions only a lucky few ever managed to experience or, for that matter, would ever want to.

Ships and yachts and boats are as often as not referred to in the feminine gender. "She rolled like a pig" is common enough maritime terminology for any vessel that behaves badly in a following sea. By the same token, "she" will often have more care, more attention, and more affection lavished on her by her male owner than a girlfriend, fiancée, or wife, and to find out why this is so you would have to dig far back into the annals of maritime history—and human psychology. From earliest times to the present day, man has frequently used the boat as a vehicle of discovery; in wandering the world's oceans, he has become once more the fetus in the womb of woman.

These masterpieces of design, no matter how large or small, how grandiose or humble, nimble or sedentary, are recognized for their one outstanding quality: the pleasure they give for the looking at. Water abhors ugliness. For the moment, the question "does it work?" is not valid here, for, as many a weathered salt will tell you, "If she looks right, she'll go right."

Within the parameters of this book, that timeworn adage is a common denominator. There are, of course, excep-

tions, as there always are with any art form or arena where current scientific technology vies with the application of the techniques of art gleaned from years of practical working experience. Further, it would be outrageous for me to suppose that every great yacht could be included in this work. Not only do the logistics prohibit such inclusion, but so too does my own subjective approach to selection. On that basis, there are bound to be favorites omitted. However, by attempting to be equally objective, I hope to have gathered a broad variety of *chefs d'oeuvre* supported by the all important and interesting detail.

There is an analogy here that art lovers may easily comprehend. Looking at yachts is much like looking at a gallery full of paintings. One goes to look to gain inspiration, to admire technique, to have one's memory jogged by composition and moved by content, to marvel at the artist's artistry and his or her experience of life. Many canvases will not move the observer to a second glance, no matter the artist; in a world of increased productivity and plastic, small boat construction, many a yacht will sail past unnoticed, no matter the designer.

In this book, the yardsticks of longevity, racing success, breakthrough in design, and beauty—but not necessarily in that order—are the key headings of selection. For this reason, it is possible that an outstanding member of, say, an Admiral's Cup team may be excluded, unless that same yacht subsequently proved successful in other important international events. A yacht that was successful for only one year but was instrumental in inspiring a new generation of yachts may well be included.

The same criteria apply largely to the selection and final choice of the designers included but do not rule out the inclusion of the genius whose yacht, although unsuccessful, inspired other designers to new paths.

We begin with the 1890s, weaving the strands of design

The Chicago Yacht Club's 12M
America's Cup challenger
Heart of America *leads the*
Yacht Club Italiano's Italia
during a match on Gage
Roads in 1986.

Left: Ydra *(center left) during 1974 One Ton race.* Opposite top: Nirvana, *designed by Dave Pedrick, leads Bob Bell's* Condor *at the start of the 1985 Fastnet. These two giants of modern ocean racing are among the many that voyage the world in search of tough competition.* Opposite bottom: Miss Alfred Marks, *a Freedom 40 yacht, sails wing and wing through a stormy Solent.*

into a loose historical framework so that cross-references are established between cruising and racing, and, importantly, to lay down the depth of pigment necessary to give a canvas life; for contrary to popular belief, winged keels and canard foils are not contemporary revolutions in naval architecture.

Three distinct periods—1890–1939, 1956–1973, and 1974 to the present day—are covered. Each of these periods saw significant developments in the field of yacht racing as well as marked and almost continual development in the field of cruising design.

Cruising design often follows closely on the heels of racing success, and this has been a common factor throughout the periods covered. Why cruising-boat designs should ape those of their racing sisters is not always clear, however, and in some instances racing design customized to meet popular taste in cruisers has not always worked effectively. The hybrid cruiser/racer is another vague area of design that has produced not just the good and the bad, but the ugly.

Ugly boats can certainly be successful, but usually only within the restrictions of a rule; it is to the rule that one must look for the cause. Here, there are no vagaries of design, only fixed parameters within which the designer must find loopholes that allow cunning, creativity, science, and experience to blossom. It is very seldom that the testing tank produces a design that is not aesthetically pleasing, even if it takes a while for popular taste to adapt.

Two classic examples are the Royal Yacht *Britannia* of the 1890s and David Hollom's radical 1986 design for an America's Cup challenger. At the time of the former's launch, observers were quick to criticize *Britannia's* ugly bow. In a long career, *Britannia* established popular affection as a direct result of her many racing successes. She became a beauty by sheer dint of winning, not because those same observers spread a word of praise concerning her elegant lines. Hollom's 12-meter challenger may well be considered ugly by some. The no-name boat was dubbed "The Hippo" by cup followers in Australia because of its supposed uncanny likeness to that animal. Look at Hollom's yacht from the right angles, and even the lay observer can see it no more resembles a hippopotamus than a giraffe resembles an ostrich. Those closest to the yacht are undecided yet as to just how fast it could be; they know it is. The main problem appears to be that the design is so radical that no one has yet discovered how to sail it properly. Hollom was called upon to design the yacht because of his expertise in model sailing yachts. *K-25*, as "The Hippo" is officially dubbed, is probably one of the prettiest 12-meter yachts to come off the drawing board for many years, but whether that means she, or her descendant, will ever compete in a future America's Cup event remains to be seen.

To my knowledge, only one yacht designer, Uffa Fox, ever achieved household recognition, and then only as the man who crewed for His Royal Highness the Duke of Edinburgh. The names of G. L. Watson, Fife, Nicholson, the Herreshoffs, Starling Burgess, Briand, Frers and Holland, Alden, Clark, and Johnson I have plucked at random from a seemingly endless list of designers selected for inclusion in this work. I would dearly love to have included more, for this book is a result of their work, the known and the unknown; their ideas, their successes and failures, their frustrations and jubilations. Anyone who can sketch a few lines on a piece of paper and then turn that two-dimensional idea into an object of three-dimensional elegance called a yacht is just as much an artist as the author of any painting hung in any gallery. And what a gallery of works these designers have created.

JONATHAN EASTLAND
Fremantle, Western Australia, 1987

CHAPTER 1

Britannia

On a fine and clear summer night some fifty years ago, the king's yacht *Britannia* slipped her moorings in the roads off Cowes and for the last time headed down the Solent under the escort of two naval destroyers, HMS *Amazon* and HMS *Winchester*. Hours later, as the light of St. Catherine's on the island's southernmost tip receded and the land merged against the darkening background of the northeast, the sad little flotilla lost way and stopped. Explosive charges placed in *Britannia*'s 43-year-old bilges were detonated. She slipped beneath the purple waves in silence.

And here, perhaps, all aficionados of yacht racing should pause for thought, for nostalgic contemplation, a little self-indulgent wistfulness for times gone by, for an era that many of us are too young to have witnessed. *Britannia*'s Viking funeral marked not only the demise of a great and beautiful ship, it marked the end of an era of yachting that had thrived on grandeur. True, there were rule changes down the years that hastened an already inevitable end to the concept of larger and more powerful yachts. But *Britannia*'s scuttling was an act of sudden finality, a marker in the pages of yachting history that points bluntly to a handful of illustrations, photographs, and paintings as the only legacy.

Left: Britannia *thunders past Cowes in 1926 with* Shamrock, Lulworth, Westward, *and* White Heather II. *Painting by Steven Dews.*

(Courtesy the Marine Gallery, Cowes) Above: *Two of* White Crusader*'s crew handle a sodden spinnaker.*

A painting by Wilson Steer, *A Procession of Yachts*, is perhaps the closest I will ever come to being moved by the grandeur, the elementary hugeness, power, and grace, of these mammoths of yesteryear, for though the legacy of photography is large, few images successfully portray the immensity of these yachts.

And they were immense: today's images of 12 meters surfing downwind pale into insignificance by comparison. While watching the two-person crew—one male, the other female—of an inflatable chase boat haul aboard a sodden spinnaker lost overboard by a 12-meter challenger in Gage Roads, I wondered how they would have coped with the gaff-topsail of *Reliance,* a Herreshoff America's Cup defender of 1903. Her topsail alone comprised more sail area than all of that of a 12 meter! And to operate this beast, some 64 tough and cussing Yankee sailors were needed.

In recent years, one or two old-timers have been salvaged from the knacker's yard or a slow and cruel death from rust and decay. Both *Shamrock V* (ex *Quadrifoglio* ex *Shamrock V*) and *Velsheda* of the J class are restored and sailing again. T.O.M. Sopwith's *Endeavour,* after a long eight-year rebuilding of her hull, was recently launched back into the Solent waters by her new owner, Elizabeth Meyer. How she managed this mammoth task will be explained later, but for the present, the launch lends scale and perspective to an understanding of just how big these big yachts were.

Her immediate previous owner, John Amos, had persuaded members of a local regiment of the Royal Engineers to help haul the 130-foot-long hulk out of Southampton Water onto a spit of sand and shingle named Calshot with the aid of several tank tractors and a specially built steel cradle. Now, with her elegant hull fully restored, *Endeavour* stood 30 feet high in the same cradle at the top of a set of greased ways.

She had erected 50 feet of mainmast to carry traditional bunting for the launch, and all around on the beach nearby sat or stood hundreds of well-wishers who had flocked from the village or Southampton city to watch what would undoubtedly be quite a spectacle.

Elegant as she is, *Endeavour*'s hull is monstrous, and when the appropriate time came for Miss Meyer to launch her in time-honored fashion, her owner became no more than a dot on the towering, pointed pinnacle of the yacht's bow.

Philip Wilson Steer painted this wonderful impression of big yacht racing at the turn of the century. (Courtesy of the Tate Gallery, London)

Opposite: *Period etching of* Britannia *winning first prize in a race at Nice in 1894.*
Right: *In this Henry Shields watercolor of 1888, the* SS Mohican *(left) acts as a marker on the Clyde during a race between the Watson-designed* Daisy, Cora, *and* Rona.
Below: Vril, *a 5-tonner designed in 1878 by Watson. Watercolor by Henry Shields.*

The Champagne bottle smashed and splintered into a thousand pieces; within a few seconds the hull was sliding and rapidly gathering speed down the shelving incline. Halfway down the ways, *Endeavour* had already traveled a distance equal to her own length. She must surely float soon. Hundreds of spectators now stood or climbed on walls and parapets to obtain a better view; cameras were half raised in anticipation while spare hands made a glare shield or covered a gaping mouth. She was still going; by now the counter and most of her keel and after ends were pushing back a wall of water six feet high. The few on-board guests and the excited owner hung on precariously to the sprawling deck as 100 tons of steel hurtled downward. Suddenly, *Endeavour* heaved up like a huge whale and rid herself of the cradle. She was afloat again after one of the most spectacular launches on the Solent for many years. It was only then that one finally had some idea of just how big and powerful those racing yachts of yesteryear really were.

Not long after *Britannia*'s scuttling, yachting writer John Irving wrote, "I remember a blustering day off the Great Nore when a venerable sea-ancient and I, side by side, watched *Britannia* lead the 'Big Class' around the triangular Mouse-Oaze-Nore Thames course. The storm scud was flying over the estuary; elusive spume hissed across short broken golden water, the Royal racing flag strained at its halyard, streaming out stiff as a board in a hardening wind. It was *Britannia*'s day—her chosen weather.

G. L. WATSON

"BONA"

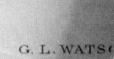

"ISOLDE."
Northern Yacht Club.

Ralston & Sons

GLASGOW.

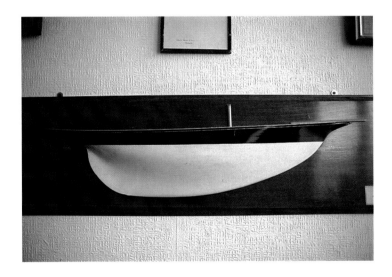

Opposite: *George Lennox Watson, Britain's most famous yacht designer.* Top: *Herreshoff's schooner yacht* Westward. *Built in 1910,* Westward *was one of the largest racing yachts of her time. Painting by Steven Dews. (Courtesy of the Marine Gallery, Cowes)* Above: *Half-model of the Watson-designed* Doris.

"In the far off 'nineties the ancient mariner at my side had sailed as a for'ard hand in her—and in many a 'crack' before that—and with a critical eye he watched the fleet round up at the mark. *Britannia* was well in the lead.

"'The old lady don't want no steerin',' he muttered. ' 'Er knows the way around, I rackon—an' how to get hoam fust as well!' "

At this time, big boat racing was almost inextricably entwined either directly or indirectly with the America's Cup, with much toing and froing across the Atlantic by wealthy English and American owners, their skippers, and yachts.

Britannia was designed by G. L. Watson and built by Henderson's on the Clyde for Queen Victoria's son Edward, Prince of Wales. In 1910 she passed into the hands of his son George V. Between 1893 and 1935 she won her royal owners 231 first prizes in 635 races. She was, and will remain, the most successful racing yacht of all time.

She was built side-by-side with the Earl of Dunraven's eighth America's Cup yacht, *Valkyrie II*, and the story goes that the Prince of Wales had approached Watson for a racing cutter to provide *Valkyrie* with competition before the cup races in the autumn of 1893.

"Look you here, Dunraven," goes the account, "If you say you are set on this American adventure of yours, I've a

Above: Satanita, *designed by J.M. Soper, leads* Navahoe *around a* Solent *course in 1893.* Left: *The 125-ton Watson-designed* Wendur *was typical of the successful cruiser/racers of her day. Note the elegant sweep of her sheer and narrow beam.* Right: *The Earl of Dunraven's* Valkyrie I, *pictured by Beken in 1890 as she thunders through the* Solent *with every stitch of canvas set and pulling hard.*

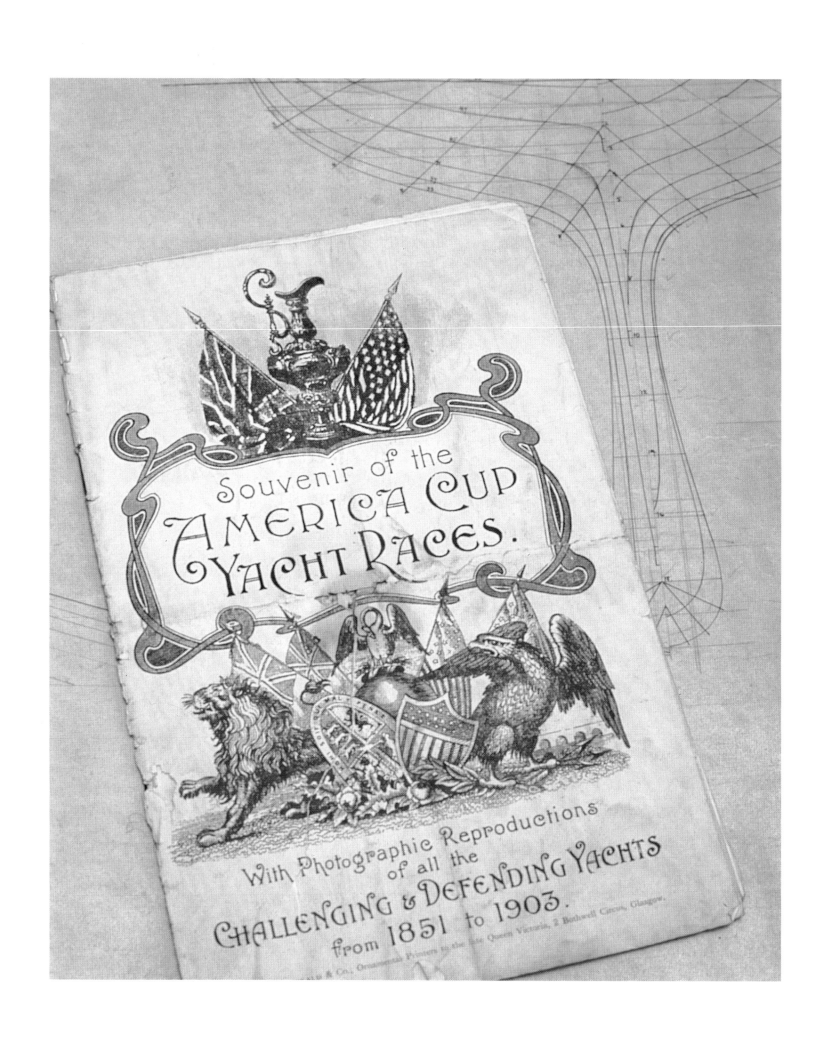

Souvenir of the
AMERICA CUP
YACHT RACES.

With Photographic Reproductions
of all the
CHALLENGING & DEFENDING YACHTS
from 1851 to 1903.

& Co., Ornamental Printers to the late Queen Victoria, 2 Bothwell Circus, Glasgow.

Opposite: *Souvenir America's Cup program rests on Watson's original sectional drawings for Valkyrie III. Above: After Britannia was scuttled, Buckingham Palace sent Watson an ashtray carved from* one of her wooden spars. Below: *Watson's wooden "sweeps," engraved with his initials: Watson used these tools to draw the fair curves of his designs.*

good mind to build something that will give your ship a chance to try herself before you sail away."

And so in due course and amid great speculation, the two huge yachts began to take shape at the former Tod and McGregor yard of David and William Henderson at the Meadowside works in Partick, Glasgow. *Britannia* was not a sistership to Dunraven's challenger, but the two had much in common—*Britannia* was, as Irving later wrote, "a cousin ship at least."

Watson was now at the peak of his career and with *Britannia* had more or less been given free rein to develop many theories close to his heart. Born in October 1851 and christened George Lennox, he was the eldest son of Thomas, a doctor, and his wife, Ellen, daughter of engineer Timothy Burstall. In 1867, the young Watson was apprenticed to shipbuilders Robert Napier and Sons after completing a fairly normal education at Glasgow High and Collegiate schools. In 1870, Watson moved to A. & J. Inglis, Clyde shipbuilders, but that was a short-lived relationship, and in 1872, George Watson began his own business in Glasgow as a naval architect.

A year later, Watson had his first success in the 5-ton racer *Clotilde*, and thereafter followed an almost legendary list of yacht names. The 90-ton *Vanduara* for John Clark was built in 1880 and immediately stole the yacht racing limelight by beating the pants off *Formosa*, owned by the Prince of Wales prior to the building of *Britannia*. *Marjorie* of 1883 cleaned up in the "big class," with the 125-ton yawl *Wendur* a close runner-up. *Yarana; Valkyrie I;* several 40 raters, including *Queen Mab*, which had a record of 31 firsts in her first season of racing; *Thistle*, an America's Cup challenger of 1887; and *Valkyrie II* followed. Watson was not only prolific, but almost everything he drew became a resounding success. He also designed many of the graceful steam yachts of the period as well as cargo, passenger, and mail steamers—a fleet of more than 450 vessels of all types by the time of his death in 1904.

In 1881, Watson read a paper at the Exhibition of Naval Architecture and Marine Engineering at Glasgow, and from it we can see how clearly he was thinking about the future of yacht design. "We have not exhausted the possibilities of form yet," he said, "and when we do arrive at perfection of shape we can set-to then and look out for better [building] material. The frames and beams, then, of my ideal ship shall be of aluminum, the plating below the waterline of manganese bronze and topsides of aluminum while I think it will be well to deck her, too, with that lightest of metals as good yellow pine will soon be seen only in museums."

Watson's concerns centered around lightness, strength, and speed. He looked at yacht design from a flying fish point of view; a hull configuration that would skim over, rather than plough through, the sea. When the Prince of Wales decided to build a new cutter, it was to Watson he turned, and Watson, after being invited to Sandringham to meet the future Queen Alexandra and discuss with the

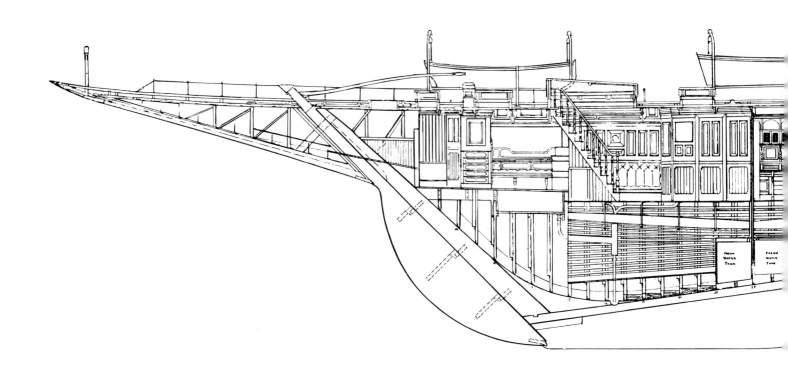

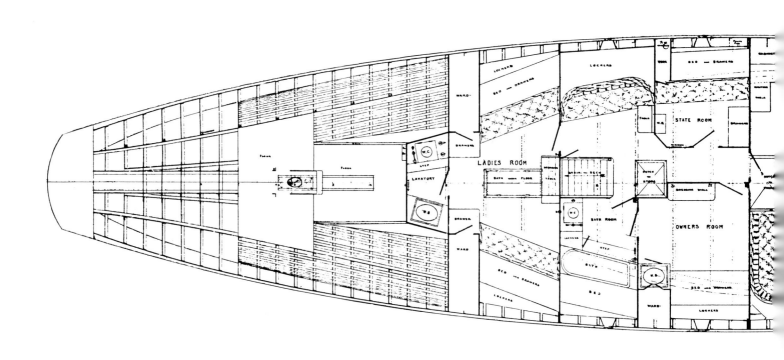

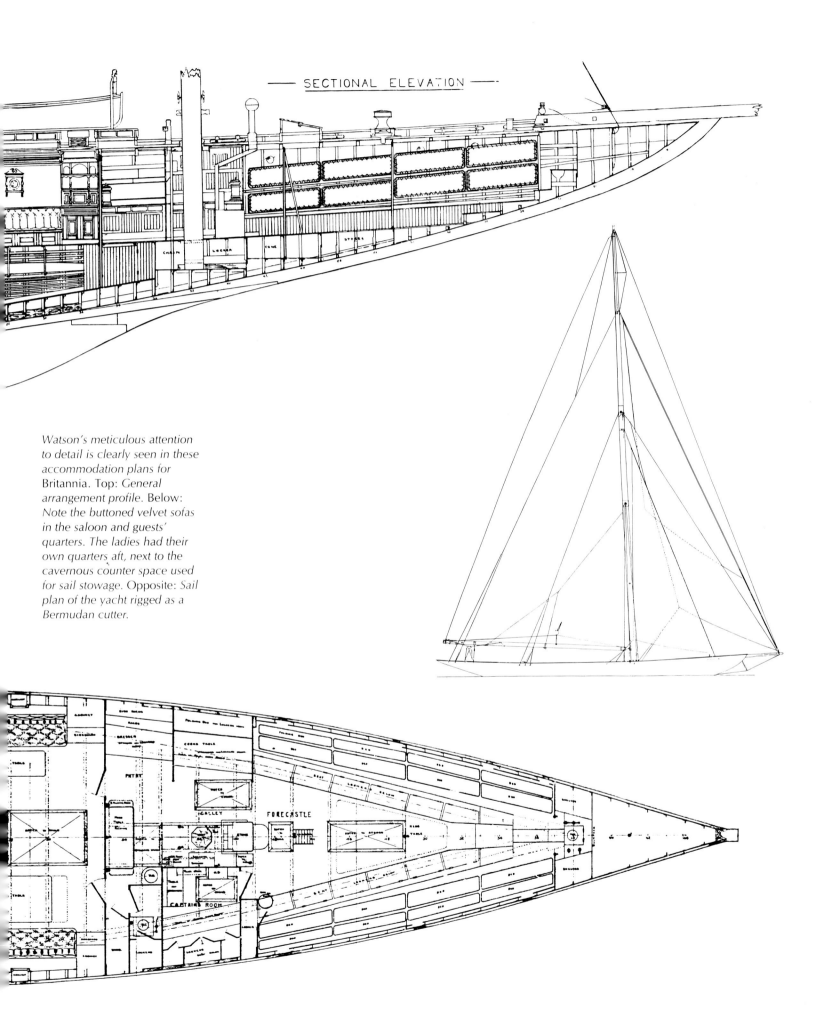

— SECTIONAL ELEVATION —

Watson's meticulous attention to detail is clearly seen in these accommodation plans for Britannia. Top: *General arrangement profile.* Below: *Note the buttoned velvet sofas in the saloon and guests' quarters. The ladies had their own quarters aft, next to the cavernous counter space used for sail stowage.* Opposite: *Sail plan of the yacht rigged as a Bermudan cutter.*

Above: *Sir Richard Sutton's* Genesta *rounding the Mouse lightship. Sutton took the yacht to America to challenge for the cup in 1885 but was beaten by the Burgess-designed* Puritan.

Opposite top: Olivette, *a Watson 3½-tonner of 1881.* Opposite bottom: Vanduara, *one of Watson's most successful racing yachts, raced around the English*

coast at major regattas on the Clyde, the Thames, and in the Solent. Watercolor by Henry Shields.

prince his new yacht, turned to his drawing board and created a masterpiece, a yacht so graceful and elegant, so fair of line, that none before or since has matched either her performance or her natural beauty.

Her overall measurements were 121.5 feet on a waterline of 87.8 feet. With a beam of 23.3 feet, her length to beam ratio was high at nearly 3.8:1. From waterline to keel bottom she needed 15 feet of clear water. She was built of American elm and pitch pine on steel frames—a composite construction much favored by designers of fast sailing ships (*Cutty Sark* is probably the most famous example)—and displaced 154 tons.

Ideally, Watson would have liked to have built *Britannia* using those same metal composites he had often talked about. His doubts about the ability of wood to withstand the enormous strains imparted on the hull by 50 tons of lead "lashing about some twelve feet below the waterline" were well known. For some other craft he had specified all-steel

construction. For the Earl of Dunraven's *Valkyrie II*, Watson opted for wood planks on steel frames, and the future king's yacht was constructed in the same manner.

A steel foundation plate was the key to successful construction; every other part of the ship would eventually be tied to it. The foundation plate was just that, and it served as a giant washer fitted to the top of the wood keel and to which was through-bolted the lead ballast keel. Vertical steel side plates were mounted to prevent lateral movement of the keel section, particularly while the yacht was driven hard in heavy seas. Steel floorplates were mounted on the foundation plate, and these held in place the transverse frames: steel sheer strakes, deck beams, and gussets stitched the whole cobweb of framing together. Keel bolts and other fastenings were cast of special metal. Each keel bolt had a breaking strain of more than 20 tons to the square inch.

Once this complicated framework was complete, planks of American elm and pitch pine were bolted to the frames

Opposite top: *Start of the Heligoland Cup from Dover in 1904 as seen by artist Charles Dixon. Brynhild (extreme left) is partly obscured by the American yacht* Ingomar *(center left). Opposite bottom: This view of the main saloon in Lady Brassey's cruising yacht* Sunbeam *shows in great detail the trappings of luxury that owners and their guests expected at sea during the 1890s. Above: Nathaniel Herreshoff revolutionized yacht design and construction techniques in the heyday of American yachting around the turn of the century.*

below the waterline. To save weight, cedar was used for the topsides. No effort was spared by Henderson's employees to ensure that each hole drilled was no larger than it needed to be, and it is a tribute to their craftsmanship that 30 years later the condition of the hull was almost as good as it had been the day it was first launched. No noticeable stretching, sagging, or expansion of joints was visible, and the yard made only minor modifications to a few frames and girders before sending the yacht off for another decade of racing. In 41 years of often hard and rigorous sailing, *Britannia's* design could not have been improved upon by anyone.

Under her original rig, *Britannia* spread some 10,000 square feet of canvas. The base of her sail plan, from bowsprit tip to the end of her boom, was 172 feet.

Even in those days, the spread of sail carried by yachts like *Britannia* was enormous and was frequently a bone of contention with yachting critics. The America's Cup defender *Vigilant* carried 11,000 square feet of canvas, and by 1903, the cup defender *Reliance* was able to spread 16,200 square feet.

In this instance, however, Watson had made not a single mistake in his calculations. Ratsey at Cowes had made *Britannia's* sails from cotton canvas, which had only recently replaced an era of heavy flax. The royal yacht's designer was well aware of the weight-saving advantages. Both hull and rig were perfectly balanced, and it is this that, combined with her fairness of line, gave her such speed and the ability to win so many races in a variety of weather conditions.

The lower mainmast was interesting, being fitted "root end" uppermost, and rose 80 feet from the deck to the capping. This section alone weighed some three tons and was always proudly presented to guests visiting the yacht by her first skipper, John Carter, as if it were one of the crew. The masts on these giant sailing yachts were constantly at risk of being overstressed, and in her first season out, *Britannia* managed to spring three such poles. A further 58 feet of topmast gave the royal yacht a sail plan that soared 142 feet above deck level. In heavy weather, the topmast could be lowered or sent down, a seamanship practice that reduced both topweight and windage and that, sadly, is not much in vogue today.

Britannia was launched on April 20, 1893, by Mrs. Henderson to cries of shock and dismay: "Her mast was stepped, her running and standing rigging sent up and her first snowy suit of Ratsey's sails was bent. At last she was ready for a trial run and tuning up under her canvas and, as she slipped her mooring and moved into open waters and the public gaze, waterside opinion and even expert opinion was unanimous in its condemnation of her ugliness."

Dixon Kemp called her newfangled bow "gratuitously ugly," but added prophetically, "The form of the stem or cutwater is a matter of taste . . . and the uneducated eye of the rising generation, untrammeled by comparisons, will grow to love the Viking stem just as past generations did the Swan stem."

And so it was to prove: the same combination of line and form that had inevitably produced the *Britannia*'s Viking bow endowed her inevitably with handiness and speed, and her bow-form, giving her forward buoyancy just where it was needed, enabled her to skim rather than plow through the seas.

Even the untrained eye cannot fail to notice the sweetness of *Britannia*'s lines. Indeed, as Uffa Fox simply illustrated many years after her launch, *Britannia*'s design was and remains a tribute to the mind of G. L. Watson. After the America's Cup defender *Enterprise* had soundly beaten *Shamrock* in 1930, Uffa took the plans of the king's yacht and over the top sketched out the lines of the American victor. The similarities were uncanny and proved beyond any reasonable doubt that Watson had long been way ahead of his adversaries and that even in later years, when the considerations of quarter beam, length, displacement, and draft were applied to the rating rules, these factors encouraged designs that, overall, bore great similarity in hull configuration to those of *Britannia*.

It was said of *Britannia* that a "better balanced and better built vessel never crossed the starting line." Watson was the genius of the age, and *Britannia*'s lines were to provide the model for designers up to the end of the J class era, her form referred to as the "*Britannia* ideal."

In those early days, much attention was paid to on-board creature comforts, and perhaps with a vessel so large, owners and designers could afford to be generous with the cavernous hull spaces.

At least half of the accommodation space in these great yachts was allocated to crew quarters and the galley. The size of the accommodation can be gauged to some degree from the illustration showing the owner's cabin aboard *Lulworth*, another old-timer that raced against some of the mighty J class and is presently the subject of a massive restoration project.

The accommodation layout of most of these period yachts is roughly similar. In *Britannia*, a huge saloon, extending the full width of the vessel, occupied the space immediately aft of the galley. Two staterooms were situated aft of the saloon and split by a central corridor and lobby at the bottom of the upper-deck stairwell. The owner's stateroom to starboard was furnished with intricately carved furniture. Thistles, roses, and shamrocks flourished in harmony with a carving of Britannia with her shield and trident.

Separated from the main accommodation by a companionway and bathroom was the "ladies cabin." Presumably, there was room for two guests in these quarters, which had their own toilet facilities and two huge walk-in hanging lockers.

The space within the pencil-thin counter served as a sail locker. This area was cleverly stiffened with a lightweight steel girder throughout its length so that the counter could withstand the enormous strains imparted by the mast backstays and boom mainsheet while hard pressed under racing canvas. "Locker" is actually an unfortunate description in this instance because it gives absolutely no idea of the warehouselike space available for sail stowage in this area.

The forthcoming America's Cup contest generated enormous interest. No fewer than nine new first-class cutters were under construction on both sides of the Atlantic that winter; Nathaniel Herreshoff designed two of the American yachts, *Vigilant* and *Colonia*. Paine of Boston produced *Jubilee*, and Starling Burgess the fourth, *Pilgrim*. Herreshoff was also responsible for Phelps R. Carroll's *Navahoe*, which crossed the Atlantic that summer to challenge in British waters for the Cape May and Brenton Reef cups won seven years earlier by Sir Richard Sutton's *Genesta*. In that season, six yachts comprised the big class; the two "Watson monstrosities," *Britannia* and *Valkyrie*; and *Navahoe*, *Culluna*, *Iverna*, and *Satanita*, the latter a J. M. Soper-designed cutter that would become the fastest of its type on a reach.

Valkyrie met *Britannia* 21 times that first summer, before the challenger headed across the Atlantic to meet *Vigilant* off Sandy Hook. *Britannia* won the first race, the Royal Thames Yacht Club River Match, on May 25. Dead level and with three miles to go to the finish off Southend, *Valkyrie*'s bowsprit snapped, and *Britannia* won by 6 minutes and 10 seconds. The record of those early races against Dunraven's yacht set the pattern for *Britannia*'s subsequent career. *Valkyrie* won 10 races, all of them in light or variable winds. *Britannia* won 8 races, all but one in fresh or heavy airs; the exception being a light airs race on July 8 that she won by the greatest margin of all—15 minutes and 39 seconds.

Despite a near full season of trials with her royal cousin, *Valkyrie* was beaten by the American *Vigilant* in three straight races; but it was a close-run thing. The following year, *Vigilant*, under captain Hank Haff, sailed to British shores and was thoroughly beaten by the royal yacht in 12 out of 17 encounters. Although the American was faster in a strong breeze, she was slower in light to moderate winds. But the members of the New York Yacht Club were so worried that they commissioned Nat Herreshoff to design a light airs flier for the 1895 cup defense. One cannot help but wonder at what might have happened had etiquette allowed *Britannia*, rather than her "near cousin," to meet *Vigilant* in 1893.

Britannia and her professional crew won 60 races during her first two seasons in 91 starts, collecting total prize money of £4,371. In 1895, she won 38 of the 50 races entered—a record she never equalled thereafter. Between 1893 and 1897, when she passed from royal ownership for the first time, this magnificent yacht managed to contribute nearly £10,000 in prize money to the formidable cost of her upkeep. But in 1897, following her royal owner's celebrated feud with the kaiser and his Watson-designed *Meteor*, *Britannia* was withdrawn from racing and sold to a Mr. J. L. Johnston of Kingswood, Sydenham—but not, ironically, before winning the kaiser's *Meteor* challenge cup outright!

Britannia looked destined to spend the rest of her days as a cruising yacht. She changed hands again—not always, perhaps, the right hands. One prospective buyer, a Mr. Hooley, cried off when he discovered that *Britannia* did not have a funnel! She was in royal ownership again in 1899 as a trial horse for Thomas Lipton's first *Shamrock*, but in cruising trim, the royal cutter was no match for the unsuccessful challenger. "Her sails were old, her copper [bottom] wrinkled, she made six starts and never won a flag." Again she was sold, this time to the king's friend Sir Richard Williams Bulkeley, a fellow member of the Royal Yacht Squadron who cruised her for two seasons from her mooring off Anglesea.

Edward VII soon tired of affairs of state, and in 1902 she was duly returned to royal ownership. For eight years, until his death in 1910, the unmistakeable cigar-puffing figure reclined in his wicker chair on the aft deck as the king's yacht toured the coastal regattas—for the most part cruising, but occasionally taking part.

In cruising trim, with increased bulwarks and wheel steering to replace her canvas-covered tiller, *Britannia* continued her career in the hands of the new king, George V. A small glass-windowed deckhouse was built over the original sliding companionway. The king's sons, the dukes of York and Windsor, freshly embarked on naval careers, spent long summer days aboard her.

Because her racing days seemed to be over for good, yacht racing lost much of its appeal for competitors and spectators alike. Then in 1913 came a royal change of heart. Under Major Hunloke, the king's sailing master and noted small boat racer, *Britannia*, still in cruising trim, entered the lists again and raced throughout that summer until at Cowes the following year came news that war had been declared. *Britannia* was again laid up in the Medina River, and *Meteor*, en route from Kiel, was hastily turned back.

The Big Class, *a classic painting by Steven Dews, shows yacht racing off Cowes in the 1930s with* Candida *and* Cambria Bermudan *rigged and* Westward *and* White Heather *gaff rigged. (Courtesy of the Marine Gallery, Cowes)*

CHAPTER 2

Progress in the Early Years

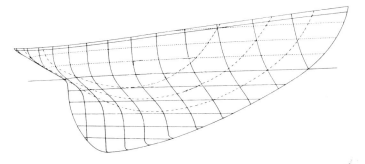

In the 1880s, long before the "horrid" bow of Watson's *Britannia* became the accepted form of elegance in yacht design, the Yacht Racing Association produced a quirky mathematical formula, viz:

$$B^2 \times (1-B) = \text{Tonnage}$$

By this rule, the powers that be measured a yacht's tonnage and assessed its racing class and time allowance.

If there is such a thing as a rule of nature in naval architecture, then it should surely be approximate and in the ratio of three to one; that is, length equals three times the breadth. In the dying years of the nineteenth century, the rule makers bent nature—and with it the formula for elegance—out of shape in their quest for speed.

Racing yachts, such as they were, became as long as eight times their breadth; a yacht of 45 feet overall might have a maximum beam of a little less than 6 feet, no more than the armspan of the average owner. Keels, on which were hung up to 70 percent of the vessel's total weight, plunged to absurd depths. Charles Nicholson's 5 rater *Dacia* measured 33.8 feet on the waterline but had a fin keel drawing 8.5 feet. Most modern naval auxiliaries based on the motor fishing–type of design rarely draw more than 9 feet for their 70-foot length!

Left: The 1870 America's Cup challenger Cambria, *restored and rigged as a ketch, racing off Western Australia in 1987. Above: Perspective drawing of* Dorade's *hull.*

Opposite: *The solidity of a 90-foot Brixham trawler epitomized seaworthy design at the turn of the century. Here, the fully restored* Provident *plunges through the Channel with every stitch of her canvas set. Right: Launch day for a Brixham trawler at the builder's yard in 1912. Note the ratio of waterline to keel depth and freeboard to deck line.*

This rule allowed designers to draw yachts of extreme length, to obtain a high natural hull speed, and simultaneously permitted almost outrageous depths of keel to compensate for the huge areas of canvas carried on relatively tiny hulls. These mostly straight-stemmed vessels were not necessarily unattractive, but nor were they elegant. Most were habitable, fitted out with interiors in a style of consummate Victorian taste; upholstered sofa-bunks, built-in mahogany vanity units, solid-fuel stove and oven, desk and writing bureau, and owner's fiddled bunk were essential items of yachting.

The young Charles Nicholson of the famed Camper & Nicholson yard at Gosport was a rising star in naval architecture at this time, exploiting the rule for all it was worth to produce yachts that would win races. If this meant that he had to depart from the commonly accepted forms of elegance to achieve the ultimate aim, Nicholson was not shy in coming forward with what were then considered ugly boats. These sailing "wedges" had humped backs—almost a reverse sheer—little freeboard, and stubby counters. Racing yacht design was as much a legacy of the common workboat configuration as it was cunning in exploitation of the rule of the period.

That cruising yacht design is often in part a legacy of the more successful racing designs of any period is probably no more clearly illustrated than by Nicholson's *Flame,* a 33-ton cruising cutter designed and built at the turn of the century that 33 years later came third in the Fastnet Race. Today, such performance from a yacht one tenth of the age that *Flame* was then would be impressive.

Flame was a narrow, deep-keeled vessel much smaller than her equally famous stablemate, *Brynhild,* a large yawl of 1899. Freeboard was minimal, but the standard of construction, fitting out, and accommodation design wanted for nothing. They epitomized "class" in the cruising yacht, and it was therefore only natural that would-be owners turned to Nicholson for more of the same. That cruising yachts could put up a perfectly respectable performance when their owners were inclined to race them against thoroughbreds of the period was due entirely to their racing pedigree. As long as that demand existed and the rule remained in force, straight-stemmed, narrow-hulled cruisers that were as wet as Niagara Falls in much more than a force 4 continued to be built well into the early 1900s and in the immediate postwar years.

At the turn of the century and earlier, scantling rules, such as those later introduced by Lloyd's for the building of racing yachts, did not exist. The result was that some "light" racers were more than a little suspect when the going became heavy. Hulls were weak and worked easily in a seaway. At this time, a cruising yacht was, by definition, a vessel used for day sailing and entertaining by its owner. Anchorages or a safe mooring were invariably reached by sunset after several hours of fast sailing. The Clyde, the Thames, and the Solent were all popular venues where, given a stiff breeze, sailing became a thoroughly enjoyable experience to be followed by dinner ashore or occasionally on board in the plush velveted surroundings of the main saloon. Owners of cruising yachts demanded a higher performance than some racer owners in terms of both construction and speed.

In Scotland, William Fife had designed and built several fast cruising vessels. *White Heather I* was a classic example. Charles Nicholson, long an admirer of Fife and anxious to establish the reputation of "class" in the south of England, began to produce and build a number of craft that had few equals.

The year 1906 saw the launch of *Nyria*, a 169-ton, 73-foot l.w.l. racing cutter. This was a one-off, not designed to any rule but Nicholson's own. She was neither pure racer nor pure cruiser, but a hybrid. Built of teak on steel frames in the composite manner, *Nyria* was classed 20 years A1 at Lloyd's. The yacht was fast, faster than the Watson-designed *Kariad* of the same year, and this was said at the time to be because of her radical bow shape—a spoonlike snout of extreme overhang that gave the hull added buoyancy and extra lift in smooth water sailing.

Nyria was a yacht designer's vision. Perhaps Nicholson had inside knowledge that the International Rule would be introduced a year after the yacht was launched. In any event, when she was entered to race in the 23-meter class

Above: *Charles Nicholson in racing attire, firmly braced behind the wheel of* Candida *as the great yacht charges through the Solent on a reach with decks awash. Opposite:* Flame, *a Charles Nicholson 33-ton cutter, featured tri-headsails and tiller steering.*

Opposite: *The common workboat configuration prevailed in offshore design until the 1930s. Custom-designed racing yachts were suited to the fair breezes and relative calm of protected coastal waters.* Right: *Owner's cabin of* Lulworth (ex Terpsichore) *built into the yacht's counter section.* Below: *Corner of the mahogany-paneled main saloon aboard* Lulworth, *complete with Napier Hemy lithograph and cutlery sideboard.*

she proved the worth of Nicholson's radical bow shape, and several other designers exploited the design. Watson's *Shamrock* and *White Heather II*, both racing thoroughbreds, outclassed the Nicholson 23-meter *Brynhild*, but the spin-off success for the southerner came in the form of *Joyette*, a 90-ton cruising ketch of undeniably elegant lines.

It may seem incongruous to some that Charles Nicholson could produce a masterpiece of cruising design and, almost simultaneously, a racing yacht so ugly it almost defied proper description. Nicholson was a great believer in exploiting the measurement rule and made no bones about it. Designing yachts to win races was his "duty"; cruising yachts allowed for a combination of creativity and proven race-winning designs. There were no rules here in which to find loopholes, only owners willing to pay for the whims of a top designer. There were plenty of such owners, and Nicholson spared no paper in drawing what he thought ought to be gracing the cruising waters of England and Europe.

Charles E. Nicholson was by no means the most prolific,

Opposite: Jolie Brise: *when she won the first Fastnet Race in 1925 she was still rigged as a Le Havre pilot cutter with loose footed sails. Five years later she was hopelessly outclassed by a new breed of ocean racing yachts.* Above: White Heather II *(center)* *racing with the fleet off Osborne Bay. Note the set of her sails and the almost flat sea. Such tall and overcanvased rigs easily caught the light breezes that often prevailed in these waters and helped make yacht racing a dramatic spectacle.*

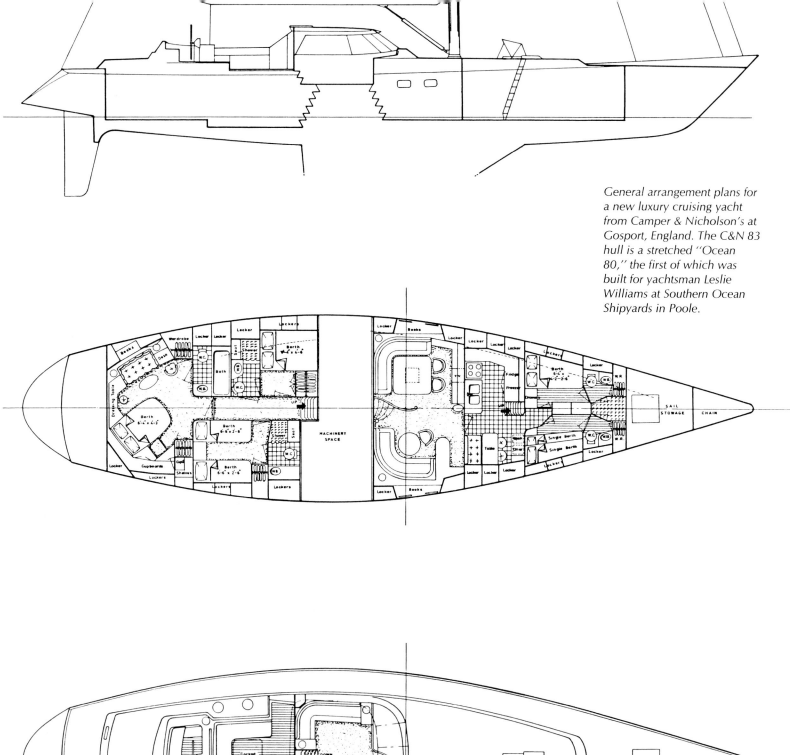

General arrangement plans for a new luxury cruising yacht from Camper & Nicholson's at Gosport, England. The C&N 83 hull is a stretched "Ocean 80," the first of which was built for yachtsman Leslie Williams at Southern Ocean Shipyards in Poole.

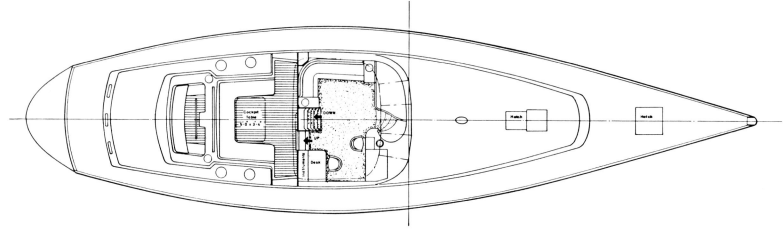

or for that matter the most artistic, of yacht designers of this period. And to broaden the picture so that all may comprehend the intricate lacework of what was really a very small and tightly knit sporting arena, the horizon must be stretched across the Atlantic, for yacht racing was inextricably involved with the grandeur of the America's Cup.

That this event—dubbed in recent years "the oldest and most prestigious of yacht racing regattas"—exists at all has to do with one thing only: money. Without the wealth that a fairly small section of society has seen fit to use to cultivate and shape the course of yachting, no racing on such an extravagant scale would have been possible.

Cruising yachts that we know today continue to be descended from successful racing types. So it was at the turn of the century and in the years after the Great War and well into the twenties and thirties. Before this, the cruising yacht as such was at best a more finely finished and lavishly appointed working boat. Just how lavish and how finely appointed depended only on the depth of one's bank account. Only the wealthy actually owned and sailed yachts at this time, and always with a fully paid professional crew. There was little scope for the less well off, the struggling baker, chairmaker, or farmer. The occasional tailor, on the other hand, might well have owned a small craft that he could sail with his family on inland waterways and lakes. Those who earned a living from the sea often took their families out "day sailing," but facilities on board a Brixham trawler, for example, were less than modest, even if such a vessel was capable of withstanding the worst that most storms could throw at it, while some custom-designed-and-built cruisers of the day could not.

In America, as in England, yacht designing had become a specialty of a handful of gifted naval architects, marine engineers, and, in a few cases, people who were simply able to draw a sweet curve. Edward Burgess of Boston was just such a person. Born in 1848, he became a self-taught draftsman and naval architect. He was an amateur who dabbled with drawing the "ideal" until, in middle age and an impecunious situation, he suddenly found supporters willing to pay for his doodles and yacht designs.

His son Starling, later to become equally famous for his work in creating a whole line of America's Cup defenders, soon joined him in business. Both of them were artists with an innate sense of what looked right must be right. Edward lacked both the theory and the practical knowledge his son was later to amass, but his instincts were uncannily right more often than not, and it is said that his blossoming late in life ultimately killed him; a seven-year period during which an uncalculable number of designs were produced followed his 1885 cup defender, *Puritan*. In the period of their great success, between 1884 and 1939, well over 2,000 sets of plans were drawn by father and son.

Starling Burgess came to yachting in a roundabout way. A dropout from Harvard, Burgess, Jr., had served as a gunner's mate in the Spanish-American War and had invented and patented a revolutionary type of machine gun. He

Above: *Steering console and wheel of the C&N 83.* Below: *The main staircase and lobby of the C&N 83 give some idea of the large amount of space for luxury accommodation aboard these craft.*

returned to Harvard and wrote three books of poetry before establishing a shipyard at Marblehead in 1905. He was undoubtedly a romantic at heart, bore a passing resemblance to Robert Louis Stevenson, and, it is said, even had a similar temperament.

In 1910, he designed and built the first plane to fly in New England, and a year later, having signed a contract with the Wright brothers, opened the first licensed aircraft company in the United States. Burgess, Jr., was also responsible for the first flying boat (the French brothers Voisin hold the distinction of having launched the first waterborne glider) to take off and land on water. Shortly afterward Burgess sold out to Glenn Curtiss (three Curtiss NC-4 flying boats made the first heavier-than-air crossing of the Atlantic in 1919) and shortly took to yacht design with Frank Paine.

Though not the first by any manner of means, the schooner Nina of 1928 was one of the most influential yacht designs to emerge in the decade after World War I. Burgess designed the 59-foot yacht for one Paul Hammond, who wanted a fast yacht to bring to England by way of a transatlantic race to Spain.

Built to the Universal Rule, Nina differed from British yachts by way of an open plan below decks and in having similar fine lines to the speedy Baltimore schooners. The same year as her launch, she entered the Fastnet Race and soundly beat all of her English opponents. She was also the first yacht to sail the Atlantic employing a Bermuda rig, a refinement of the Marconi rig developed by Charles Nicholson in 1912 for the 15-meter Istria and so-called because of the mast's aeriallike appearance.

For her 50 feet of waterline length, Nina carried 2,300 square feet of sail on a beam of a little over 15 feet. Her great success was due in no small part to the lightweight hull devoid of the fashionable encumbrances still much sought after for the purpose of comfort in English yachting circles. Her rig also played a major part, and it is strange that Nicholson's earlier experiments with Istria and later with his one-off Nyria were not more widely accepted by the pure racing fraternity in Europe. Needless to say, after Nina had visited English shores and played havoc with the winnings, only a handful of gaff-rigged topsail yachts were to be seen the following season. By 1935, there was not a crack racer that was not Bermudan rigged.

Nina remained competitive right up until the outbreak of World War II and in 1940 sailed in the last offshore race from Block Island to Gloucester, Massachusetts. Twenty-two years later, the same yacht became the oldest ever to win the Bermuda Race, a feat that not even her designer might have thought possible.

The fact that she won the race that year is indicative of how slow moving the march of progress in yacht design had become. Furthermore, this was a period often described as the heyday of yachting in England. It was the great fleets of 12-, 8-, and 6-meter yachts that drew the attention of the public, and, for the most part, yacht racing was still pretty much confined to racing around the buoys.

Opposite: Dorade was an Olin Stephens masterpiece, a design for an ocean racer that employed many of the designer's thoughts and experiences from racing smaller, 6-meter yachts. Dorade became a benchmark in yacht design. Above: Starling Burgess (left) with Harold S. Vanderbilt on deck of Rainbow.

The first Fastnet Race, an "offshore" event of over 600 miles, did not take place until 1925, and the seven yachts that started were all converted working craft of one sort or another. That year's winner, *Jolie Brise*, was a 55-foot Le Havre pilot cutter; no such thing as an "ocean racing yacht" existed outside of America, where long-distance ocean racing had started before World War I in 1906 with the Bermuda Race and the transpacific race to Honolulu.

In Europe, deep sea, or "ocean," races did not appear on the yachting calendar until after the first Fastnet had been sailed. The competitors of that race formed the Ocean Racing Club, later to become the Royal Ocean Racing Club, and in 1928 held the first Channel Race over a course from Southsea to Le Havre and back. The Cowes to Dinard Race had come about after King Edward VII presented a challenge cup in 1906 to the Club Nautique de la Rance for a race for yachts of over 30 tons, but the first race was not actually sailed until 1913, and regular Dinard races began to take place annually only from 1930.

There may not have been any crack racers without a Marconi rig by 1935, but we can now begin to see some of the reasons why the rate of progress in offshore design went along at a drifter's pace. When *Jolie Brise* entered the Bermuda Race of 1932, having sailed the Atlantic on her own bottom to start with 26 others, she was still gaff rigged and still epitomized the best that Europe could offer at this time. She never completed the race, having gone about to the aid of a burning competitor and returned to Montauk with her cargo of survivors.

The Americans were well ahead in the design of offshore craft by now. *Nina's* success of 1928 in the Fastnet was followed by an even more devastating blow to British morale when the Stephens brothers, Olin and Rod, arrived in English waters with *Dorade* in 1931 and outraced 16 other entries in that year's Fastnet by such a wide margin that the brothers and their crew were given a ticker-tape welcome on returning to New York.

The Stephens brothers had formed a partnership with Drake Sparkman in the spring of 1928 and by the time of their clean sweep with *Dorade* were probably one of the most successful and influential firms of yacht designers in the history of modern yacht racing, and they continued to be so well into the 1970s.

Because the Sparkman and Stephens partnership is so well known, it often overshadows other equally important designers whose earlier works are of particular interest and more clearly show the direct links between "agricultural" yachting and the cruiser/racer types of the day.

In Victorian times, working class families went "yachting" on tarred and hemped fishing craft. The better off cruised on lakes and inland waterways. This delightful Norfolk Broads scene would have looked very similar a hundred years ago.

CHAPTER 3

Sacrificing Speed for Seaworthiness

While Nicholson, Burgess, and later Olin Stephens much preferred the "slack bilge" and deep-keel "yacht" hull and shared a primary interest in racing, there were many, many people whose pockets could ill afford the expensive luxury of finely finished craft with steam-bent frames and polished brightwork. Furthermore, while appreciating the obvious values of a faster hull, they were more concerned with whether their ideal hull would be comfortable on long passages that might experience a variety of weather conditions.

During the post–Great War years in Europe, yachting was confined pretty much to racing around the buoys in the Solent and other traditional venues such as the Thames and the Clyde. In America, there was a growing demand for substantial cruising yachts capable of making distant voyages up and down the East Coast to the Florida Keys and even farther afield, on occasion to the Caribbean, Europe, and North Africa.

A number of designers on both sides of the Atlantic were already well noted for their work in this field, producing plans that were, to all intents and purposes, not much more than workboats fitted with accommodation. In America, a young self-taught naval architect by the name of John G. Alden—"John O' Boston" to those who knew him well—was struggling to become established.

The modern Alden 44, designed
for comfortable cruising.

Opposite: *John G. Alden, one of the 20th century's most prolific yacht designers, often sacrificed speed in his quest for seaworthiness.* Right: *Helm position of an Alden 50; the Alden 50 incorporates many of Alden's concepts of comfort afloat.*

Alden was born John Gale at Troy, New York, on January 24, 1884. He was one of four children who survived out of eight born to his mother, Mary. His father was a lawyer. Very little salt ran in his parents' blood, but by all accounts they were concerned to give their offspring a taste of the different life and could afford a summer home at Sakonnet, Rhode Island. The house was at Warren Point, a stone's throw from the water's edge of Long Pond, and it was here that John G. got to messing about on the water with his sister Antoinette and the neighbors' children.

From a very early age, Alden carved model yachts and sketched just about every boat he saw. His drawings covered scraps of paper, notebooks, or anything that came conveniently to hand. He would spend hours whittling away at lumps of wood, producing wonderfully detailed hulls from his sketches of vessels he had seen in the harbors nearby that had taken his fancy. He seemed to have a natural talent in this creative direction, and it eventually blossomed into a skill and a habit that were never to leave him.

By the time he was 12, Alden's knowledge of current trends in yacht design was formidable. Old-timers who gathered on the shore at Warren Point to watch the America's Cup matches were once given a lecture by Alden on every dimension of each of the yachts taking part. He apparently also had an expert knowledge of how each yacht performed in any given weather condition and how each skipper would handle his craft.

With his elder sister Antoinette, Alden's introduction to the way of a boat began with a flat-bottomed punt that he attempted to sail with an umbrella. When he was 10, his parents gave him a catboat, and later he progressed to a larger craft measuring 21 feet in length modeled on the Dorchester Bay dory. Rather than have the builder deliver this craft to Rhode Island, Alden took delivery at Troy and then sailed the tiny vessel down the Harlem and East rivers, up Long Island Sound, and along the coast to Sakonnet. It was a hazardous voyage, and he nearly didn't complete it after the vessel had sprung one or two strakes. He eventually docked safely after a three-week cruise and later proceeded to sail this half decker around the bay in a 40-knot breeze to satisfy the whim of a bet.

By the turn of the century, John Alden had learned more than most men his age about sailing small craft. The family moved from Troy to Dorchester and later to Boston, where his father died. Rather than continue his academic education at college, John Alden set out to train as a naval architect. He joined the firm of Edward Burgess as a messenger.

Edward's son Starling was at this time running the office, but Alden's habit of doodling on any free drawing board in between running errands was too much. Alden left by mutual agreement and went to work for B. B. Crowninshield, a renowned designer with a particular interest in working schooners. His Gloucester schooners were famous for their speed and seaworthiness. After a year as an unpaid

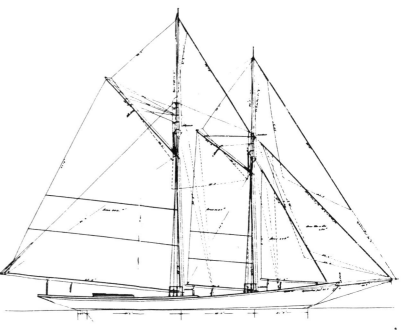

Left: Bluenose, *designed by W. J. Rove in the 1920s, was arguably the most famous Grand Banks schooner ever built.* Above: *Line plans for* Tartar. Opposite: Tartar *in action.*

Opposite: Fame:

apprentice, Alden was finally given a drawing board of his own on which he worked on the lines of two schooners, the 130-foot sisterships *Tartar* and *Fame.*

Some years later, Alden took a scratch crew up to Halifax to recover *Fame,* which was in danger of having a writ slapped on its mast for contravention of Canadian fishing regulations. The voyage back to Boston was fraught with near disasters, but eventually the 130-foot schooner reached port with the 23-year-old Alden sharing command with an old sea-dog captain nearly three times his age.

In 1908, Alden married Helene Harvey, and a year later their first child was born. Alden had spent nearly eight years working for Crowninshield on a meager salary, drawing many of the firm's famous schooners. He had worked on the lines of *Fame,* and perhaps that was one of the reasons

he had felt so confident about taking the vessel out of harbor in the dead of winter and driving her into the teeth of not one gale, but several. His experiences during the voyage to Boston were such that far from being disillusioned by the performance of *Fame,* Alden had been impressed by the vessel's great sea-keeping qualities, her durability under stress and a weight of canvas; so impressed was he that the influence of these early years is much in evidence in many of his subsequent designs.

At first, Alden's success as a yacht designer was somewhat stifled; business was slow in coming, and consequently there was little room for expansion of the firm. He had only one draftsman and a portfolio of some 50 designs. With a war in Europe looming ahead, he began to produce designs for patrol vessels, but none of these was ever built.

One or two private orders for schooners, a motor yacht, and a huge 150-foot commercial coasting schooner just kept the wolf from the door, until, when war did finally arrive, he closed the business and enlisted in the army.

When the Great War ended and Alden was discharged, he returned to designing at the office he had set up on State Street in Boston. His greatest talents were that he could sketch a potential customer's "ideal" yacht on a paper napkin in a few minutes and that he was a great seaman. His sales ability was unquestionable. With such natural abilities, it was not surprising that the more mundane tasks of drawing out the lines of a yacht were left to people more adept at interpreting his ideas into builder's plans. Alden would periodically walk around his growing domain of drawing boards and add a penciled line wherever he

thought necessary. Ideas for new boats came from lengthy discussions with his staff and ever-increasing list of customers. As the portfolio of designs proliferated, Alden would suggest that aspects of drawings already completed be used for working up new boats with modifications to ends, rig, and accommodations where the customer had indicated preferences.

With yacht brokerage and insurance added to the functions of the business, Alden was able to speculate by commissioning the occasional yacht from lesser-known yards that were normally engaged in building fishing vessels. These yards produced competently finished hulls, even if they lacked the finesse of more up-market establishments. That was of no matter to Alden, since many of his customers could ill afford the luxury of polished bright-

work. What they wanted was a yacht that could go to sea in a gale of wind and wouldn't cost the earth or a second mortgage to build.

Until the early twenties, John Alden had produced most of the company's drawings himself; however, as more and more commercial work came his way and as yachting magazines began to feature his new designs, Alden hired more people to get the drafting work completed in time to meet builders' production schedules. Much of the success of his business was due in part to the efficient team he gathered on State Street, a team that included secretary Ethel Bacon, who in the years to come virtually took over the smooth running and general administration of the business. Alden allowed Bacon a free hand, preferring to spend time visiting the many yards building his designs.

Until his retirement in 1955, when the Alden company was bought by Donald Parrot and two friends, Bill Anderson and Joseph Whitney, John Gale Alden had masterminded some 900-odd yacht designs. There were probably many more than this in actual fact, and if one were to add all the designs he produced for government contractors for commercial ships and small work craft, the design list would be twice as long.

Like many designers before him, and many who were to follow, Alden reaped his rewards from a "golden age," a period during which many of his designs saw considerable success in the racing arena despite the fact that they were not really out-and-out racing machines.

His most successful yachts were the Malabars, a line of thirteen schooners, ketches, and yawls in the 40–50 foot range. Over a period of 20 years, these famous yachts were to keep Alden at the top of the seagoing yachtsman's list. The Malabars were speculative commissions built for the designer's pleasure as much as to advertise his skills. In consecutive ocean races, particularly the Bermuda Race and the Onion Patch series, these craft came to epitomize all that was good in an Alden design, no matter whether one owned an Alden catboat or a 130-foot cargo coasting schooner.

At this time, the mid twenties, ocean racing was still pretty much in its infancy. Almost a decade was to pass before radically different craft from the drawing boards of other designers were to begin sliding down the ways to have a new impact on the world of yacht racing.

Alden's schooners, and most of the Malabars, were schooner rigged, either topsail or bald headed, and were all closely related to the earlier Gloucester-type vessels he had worked on during the early days with Crowninshield. These

were fishing schooners for which Alden had enormous admiration. *Malabar I,* which came to fruition in 1921, was modeled on just such a fishing schooner that had itself been modified to personal taste by its builder, Charles A. Morse of Thomaston, Maine.

Alden developed a useful relationship with the Morse yard. The first Alden Malabars were built at what would certainly be considered a favorable cost price, a policy that helped the builder because it ultimately brought more work through the racing successes of Alden's work. The policy undoubtedly helped Alden too in these early years of postwar work. Luckily, both builder and designer had already established a useful working relationship through much earlier work that Alden had first begun for Morse nearly a decade before.

To say that Alden copied the existing lines of successful working craft would be a falsehood. As an artist—and he was an artist in the true sense of the word—Alden always had his own ideas of how a vessel should look. He admired any vessel that boasted lines of elegance and always endeavored to ensure that his own draftsmen produced lines that were "sweet." But beauty for the sake of it was not enough. Alden wanted boats that could sail in a stiff breeze and not have to run for shelter every time a squall loomed

Opposite: Malabar III. Above: Malabar II. Malabars II *and* III *were schooner rigged, their lines developed from ideas Alden gleaned from sailing on and observing Gloucester fishing schooners.*

Opposite: *The Alden 54 has a neat chain pipe arrangement with fairleads set into the toe rail capping, a workmanlike approach to seamanship.* Above: *Melonseed duck boat replica under construction at Mystic Seaport. This is typical of the small craft in which Alden learned the rudiments of sailing and hull design.* Below: *The navigation and chart table station on the Alden 54 demonstrate a practical approach to ergonomic design.*

on the horizon; he wanted craft that could be sailed short-handed on long-distance voyages; that required a rig that could be easily handed in almost any weather condition.

Alden had a total disdain for yachts that sailed on their ear, a legacy from some earlier experience of owning and sailing a narrow-gutted "lead mine" that would perform only with the lee rail partially submerged. *Malabars I to IV* were high prowed with beautiful, sweeping sheerlines. Alden's creativity incorporated the best qualities of certain working craft and cleverly incorporated these lines into his own very original designs, designs that were to multiply into hundreds over the years to come.

Gradually, because Alden's office was busy producing innumerable other designs for customers in tandem with his own personal requirements, the Malabar series became less workmanlike in appearance. The essence of the yacht is noticeable in the finer entry of *Malabar V,* of which Alden's professional skipper was later to opine that no better boat could be designed. When number VI came off the builder's stocks and had been sailed awhile, Alden agreed.

Alden's yacht designs were essentially and firstly for the purpose of cruising, even though Alden was an avid racing enthusiast. There are very few of the 900 designs that do not show the Alden characteristic—a unique blend of fullness in the bow sections combined with fair, subtle curves running back to the belly and out to a natural progression at the counter. This became something of a trademark by which each could be recognized in an instant, no matter whether it be a ketch, schooner, or day sailer. Seaworthiness was of parmamount import to Alden, and he developed this trait to the extent that it can be seen even in shallow-draft motor launches designed primarily for use on inland waterways.

Naturally, there were variations on this theme. *Malabar XII,* for example, was a ketch. Alden told his draftsman Carl Alberg to ignore any rating rules that were then in force as he had no intention of racing the yacht. This 46 footer was built by the Morse Boatbuilding Corporation (formerly C. A. Morse), a fact that may explain why her sections are so much fuller and rounder than some earlier Malabars. The influence of those early fishing schooners is right back in evidence.

The Malabars were cruised extensively and raced as often as time would allow. One of Alden's favorite long-distance events was the Bermuda Race, in which the Malabars and other Alden designs invariably performed magnificently, bringing home class and line honors trophies. As the Bermuda event was a very popular race, Alden's reputation as a designer of fast, safe, and seaworthy craft soon spread. After a season or two of successful racing, the Malabars joined the company's brokerage lists, where they were soon snapped up by admiring friends or yachtsmen who could not wait for a sistership to be built. When one was retired, another would soon slip down the ways of a favored builder's yard and be ready for the start of a new season, with "John O' Boston" anxious to get behind the

Left: *Deck view of* Eleuthera II, *a 56-foot Alden ketch which was a direct descendant of* Minots Light, *herself a development of* Malabar XIII. *Opposite:* Minots Light *epitomized all that was elegant in a John Alden design. Built by Abeking & Rasmussen in Hamburg, the yacht was used by yachtsman and author Arthur Beiser and his family for 17 years of voyaging.*

wheel. These boats, drawn by Alden and sailed in every sort of weather with the designer at the helm, were the best advertisement he could have had.

While probably better known for his schooner yachts, Alden was nevertheless a prolific designer of many other types. From the beginning, he drew and had built a number of one-design yachts, including the ubiquitous Q class, which were as ugly as sin out of the water and more or less equally so in it. The sheerline went from a sweeping shallow curve from the counter to just for'd of amidships, where it began a slender reverse. At the time, the Universal Rule encouraged long, drawn-out ends and an almost 5:1 beam to length ratio. These boats were as wet as fish in anything more than a slight chop. The Q boat was a 25 rater, and Alden had a lot of time for the class even though its demise was not long in coming. He designed five altogether, of which two were for his own use in regattas held at Marblehead.

Other racing designs included the Nantucket One-Design, which was a centerboard day sailer, and the Pequot-Black Rock One-Design, a day sailing keelboat designed especially for the yacht club of the same name on Long Island Sound. This had also originally started life as a centerboarder. The Southern California Bird Class was yet another peculiar one-design, built for sailing on San Francisco Bay, with the first of its type built in 1922. The Stamford One-Design came even earlier, in 1916, and was

essentially a knockabout with sweet and very pleasing lines.

Others included the Bermuda One-Design and, naturally, perhaps, the Sakonnet One-Design, which was designed for the yacht club there, where Alden had learned to sail as a boy. He enjoyed these keelboats immensely and had two of his own at various times. The U.S. One-Design was much more the thoroughbred racing machine, and some thirty-odd boats were built in open and doghouse version by the Quincy Adams Yacht Yard at Quincy, Massachusetts.

Alden's commercial work was somehow fitted in between a massive drafting work load shared in the office by Carl Alberg, Frank Mather, and others. Designs for luxury motor yachts and motor sailers and ideas for a wide variety of other craft all had to be fitted into the schedule, such were the demands on Alden's talent. Few other designers have contributed as much as he to the tapestry of yachting.

While Alden's Malabars are perhaps his best-known designs, there came subsequently many others that would, in my view, be entitled to share equal acclaim, and if one looks carefully at Alden's vast collection, there are probably many that he might have designed for his own use had time permitted. One such is a cruising yacht that actually caused Alden some grief during his later years but that gave at least one man enormous pleasure for nearly two decades.

Minots Light is a ketch designed in 1950 for Clarence

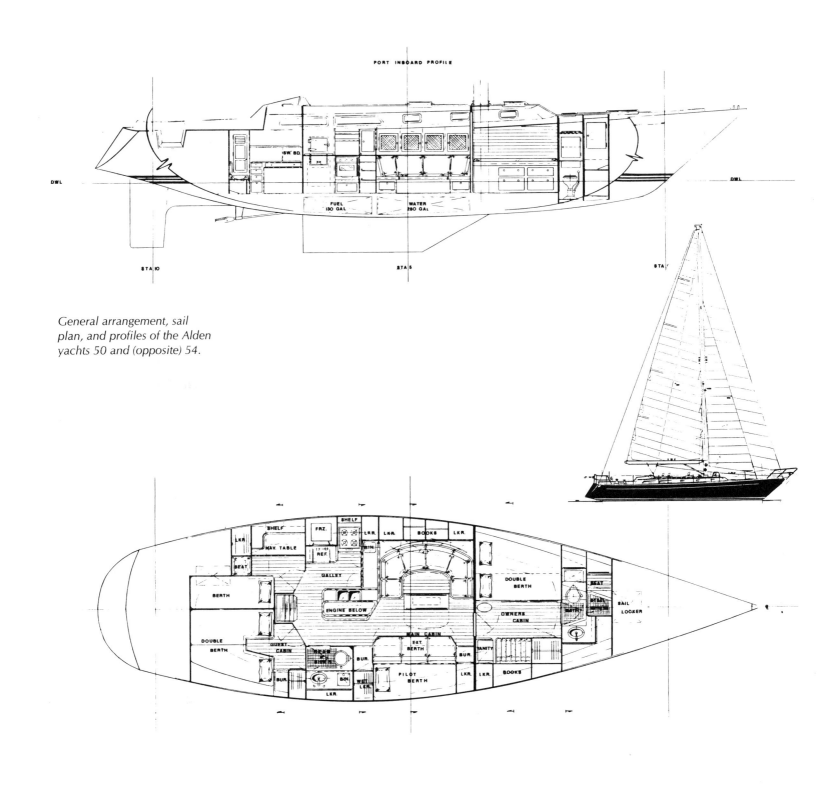

PORT INBOARD PROFILE

General arrangement, sail plan, and profiles of the Alden yachts 50 and (opposite) 54.

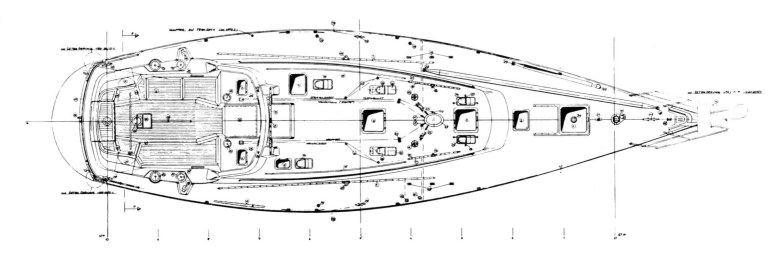

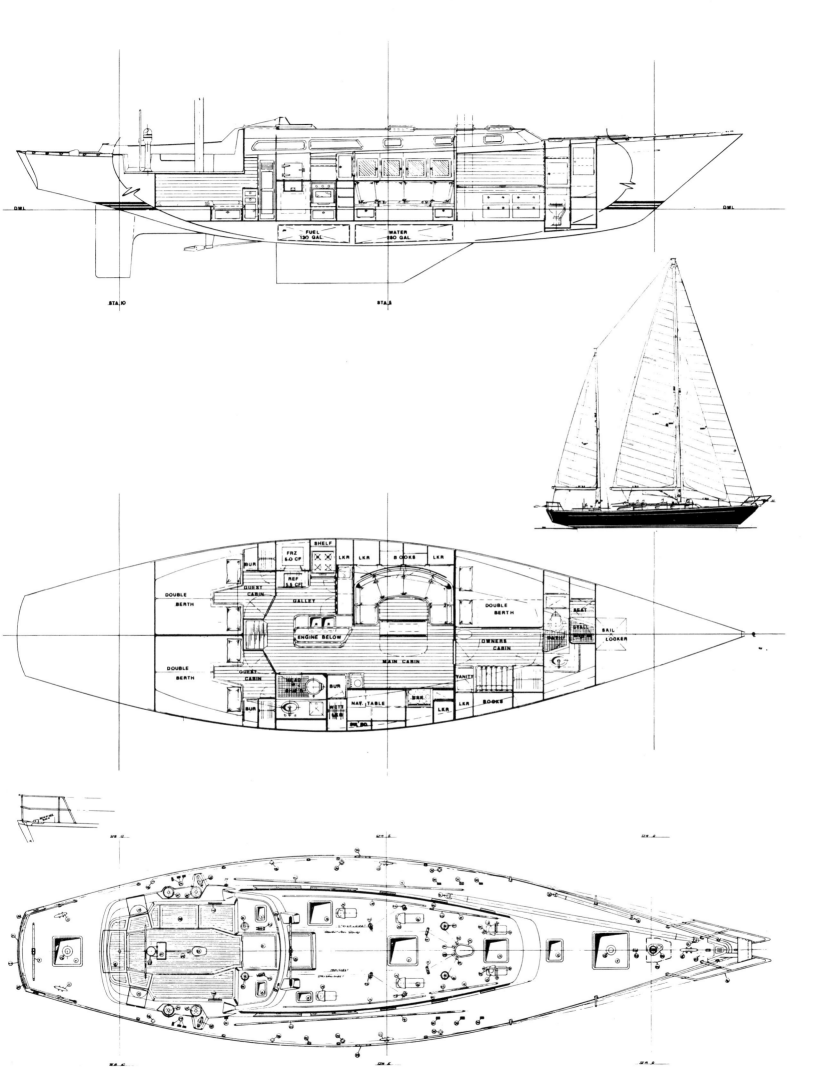

FUEL
130 GAL.

WATER
280 GAL.

DWL

STA.10

STA.5

SHELF

FRZ.
5.0 CF

LKR

LKR

BOOKS

LKR

BUR.

GUEST
CABIN

REF.
5.5 CF

GALLEY

DOUBLE
BERTH

DOUBLE
BERTH

ENGINE BELOW

OWNER'S
CABIN

DOUBLE
BERTH

SEAT

STALL

SAIL
LOCKER

MAIN CABIN

DOUBLE
BERTH

GUEST
CABIN

HEAD

VANITY

BUR.

BUR.

NAV. TABLE

BAR

LKR

BOOKS

BUR.

WET LKR

Warden. Alden sailed on the yacht in the Onion Patch of 1954 when he was 70 years old but had difficulty negotiating the deck. To Alden's great distress, he was not allowed to take the helm. Had he lived longer, Alden would have gotten great pleasure knowing that a young college professor by the name of Arthur Beiser subsequently took ownership and with his wife and young family spent the next 17 years cruising to Europe, the Mediterranean, the West Indies, and the eastern seaboard of the United States. Her owner describes *Minots Light,* in his book *The Proper Yacht,* as "the almost perfect yacht."

Built by Abeking & Rasmussen of West Germany, the 58-foot ketch has a welded-steel hull with teak-laid decks on steel frames. Her fully laden displacement is some 64,000 pounds or 28.5 tons. A 100 horsepower General Motors diesel can push the yacht along at 9 knots, but her sailing speed has been faster, if somewhat modest by the present-day standards of some oceangoing vessels.

Beiser says he bought *Minots Light* to satisfy a dream. He had first seen her while cruising on the East Coast in 1957, and the way in which she had stood out from the rest of the craft moored about her became a constant thorn in his side. "The more I looked at her, the more perfect she seemed." Every cruise that he and his family subsequently made in the yacht could have been easily accomplished in a vessel of smaller dimension. Beiser could have found any number of reasons for ridding himself of a financial burden, for there is no romance about the finances of owning a large yacht.

No, *Minots Light* is a combination of many things. She sails well and fast, is easily controlled by a shorthanded crew, is strong and seaworthy and big and beautiful. She is an Alden *chef d'oeuvre*—a work of art that anyone appreciating such quality would want to own.

A similar design that followed four years later and was launched as *Eleuthera II* bears a striking resemblance to *Minots Light.* The former was two feet longer and, aside from being similarly ketch rigged, looks almost identical to the latter. But look again. *Eleuthera II* has a straighter stem, entry is finer, and buttock lines less full. *Minots Light* really is almost perfectly shaped, as beautiful out of her element as in. And once again the observer can see the pedigree, that familiar "Gloucester line" so evident in the Malabars of the 1920s. She was, in fact, a development of *Malabar XIII,* not quite the last of the line, but one with a fine racing record.

Alestra, an Alden 50, shows off her clean lines in a stiff breeze. Plenty of light reaches below decks accommodation through well-positioned portlights and hatches.

CHAPTER 4

Pursuing the Illusory Ideal

Half a century before John Alden was born, Julia Walker gave birth to a boy. One of five children born in the tiny hamlet of Tolderodden on a rocky promontory overlooking Larvik Fjord in Norway, Julia Walker was the wife of William Archer, a timber merchant who had emigrated from Scotland some years previously. They already had a large family; seven children were born in Fifeshire on the Firth of Tay. The new arrival at Tolderodden was named Colin. He was born far too early for the period covered by this work, but his inclusion is valid because the legacy of his work continues to influence cruising yacht design in a unique manner. His designs for working craft, particularly pilot vessels, were modifications of a type of fishing vessel much in use on the southern coast of Norway near Oslofjord.

Colin Archer spent his childhood in a community of shipowners. The local menfolk were mostly seafarers; those who weren't were chandlery owners or shipping agents. The southern coast of the country thrived on the foreign and not inconsiderable coasting trade that plied across the North Sea and down to Europe and the Mediterranean.

It was perhaps not surprising then that the young Colin showed enormous interest in all that was going on around him, particularly as his father had become a lobster merchant, director of a local firm of timber merchants, and was generally considered a pinnacle of the local establishment.

Left: Venus, *a modern-day replica of a Colin Archer design.* Above: Scenery typical of the coastline near Oslofjord *where Colin Archer practiced his craft. Note the double-ended rowing skiffs.*

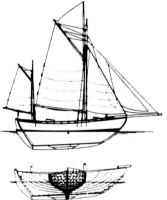

Above: *Archer's first Redningskoite pilot cutter, fully restored to sailing trim.* Left: *Archer based many of his ideas for safer fishing and pilot boats on his wave form theory. The lines show designs for a Redningskoite pilot cutter of about 36 feet.* Opposite: *Colin Archer, who devoted most of his life to designing seaworthy workboats and yachts.*

When his schooling was finished, the young Archer went to work as a carpenter across the fjord at Treschow, where a friend of William Archer's ran a shipyard. In the meantime, his elder brothers had been packed off to Australia to find a new life and, it was hoped, wealth. Australia was then a new and somewhat boisterous nation, and many Scots families sent their offspring there, figuring, perhaps, that the six-month voyage to Perth would prepare their young minds for much of what lay ahead.

Colin Archer's employment at the Treschow shipyard lasted only long enough for him to learn the essentials of the shipbuilding trade. In 1850 he was shipped off to Australia by way of California, where he stopped to go prospecting for gold with his brother Tom. Two years later, he set sail for the Hawaiian Islands, where another brother, Archibald, owned a plantation. Finally, he reached Australia and went to live with four other brothers who were sheep farmers in New South Wales.

Colin Archer might have spent the rest of his life in the new colonies had sad news not arrived from Norway eight years after his arrival. The boys' father, William, was in ailing health and unlikely to last much longer. Colin was dispatched homeward, and while on the way, he received further tragic news that his elder brother Charles had died following a skiing accident. Colin Archer arrived at Tolderodden to find himself head of the family. He was to stay for the rest of his long life, and in so doing he made a unique contribution to the world of sailing and in particular to yacht design.

Colin Archer had had no formal training in naval architecture and, aside from the eighteen months spent at Treschow as a carpenter, knew little of the intricacies of ship design. He was an experienced sailor, though, and a keen one. For a few years after his return from Australia, in between managing the family fortunes he would spend hours on the fjord sailing in small open boats.

It was probably during just such an outing that he decided to take up naval architecture and shipbuilding as a career. Many of his hours afloat were spent watching how other craft performed. One of his greatest concerns was that local fishermen were constantly being drowned when their open boats capsized in rough weather. A few fishermen had adopted a partially decked version, and this was also in use by local pilots who struggled throughout the year in all kinds of weather to find and board foreign and coastal square riggers and bring them safely into port.

The Hvalerbaat was a relatively shallow draft vessel with little sheer; pointed at both ends but bluff bowed, these little ships sailed well enough in reasonable weather. When the high, short, and choppy seas came in winter, they pounded heavily, often made no headway at all, and frequently had their planks stove in by shifting ballast. Although that was probably the worst that could happen—apart from total loss and consequent death of man and boy, for the pilot boats were crewed by only two—life aboard these 28 footers must have been precarious.

Colin Archer

The Hvalerbaat, or Whale Island boat, as it was sometimes called, was of lapstrake construction, built lightly for speed. For their length, their beam ratio was about 3:1 with shoal draft of 3 feet. All the ballast was internal and rarely secured properly. In winter, the half decks and gunwhales iced up, creating a treacherous rink on which the pilot had to dance in order to get his ship. The light construction and heavy pounding caused the decks to work, so the boats leaked like sieves; their below-deck accommodation was enough to stoop in, and while some sported solid-fuel stoves, the conditions pilots and fishermen endured were appalling.

Colin Archer spent much of his day hunched over a drafting board. J. Scott Russell, the brilliant Scots engineer responsible for the lines of Brunel's *Great Eastern*, had evolved a theory of the wave line after spending considerable time studying the formation and effect of waves on a hull. Brunel's great ship was designed to some extent around this theory. The theory made some sense in principle, and from it a set of lines for a ship could be drawn in which certain lines of the vessel were related to the shape of waves.

Still studying the elements of naval architecture, Archer took Russell's theory one stage further by evolving the wave form theory. Both theories were in fact of little practical use, as later architects were to prove. They did, however, contribute largely to the elimination of the age-old principle adopted by ship designers for generations, that of the "cod's head and mackerel tail" assimilation, much favored from before Elizabethan times through centuries of shipbuilding.

The theories evolved by Russell and Archer encouraged finer forward entries, and while Russell's *Great Eastern* was pretty much a flop, even though from an architectural and

Left: *This view of the modern Norwegian-built Overseas 35 clearly shows the influence of Archer design, much favored in Scandinavian countries.*
Above: *Pluto, a Johnson-designed 28 footer, under construction using the strip-plank method at Lou Lou's Marine in the West Indies.*
Below: *Interior view of the galley area and main saloon of the Overseas 35; it lacks the openness of some contemporary designs for this type of craft.*

Paul Erling Johnson—ocean wanderer, yacht designer, and artist—at the tiller of his yacht Venus, which was built as a sister yacht to Moon and was constructed of fiberglass using the Airex foam sandwich technique.

engineering viewpoint it was way ahead of its time, Archer stubbornly refused to give way, believing that his ideas would be of enormous benefit to the Larvik community.

He set out to prove these theories by building several modified lapstrake Hvalerbaats in a tiny shed erected at Tolderodden. The lapstrake principle of building wooden craft obviated the need for caulking between planks. As soon as the boats settled in the water, planks would swell and form a watertight seam. But for the practical purposes of a pilot boat—hardworking craft that took a continuous bashing against the sides of much larger vessels—the lapstrake principle was of little value.

Colin Archer explained his theories to skeptical pilots as well as to the occasional fisherman, pointing out the economic value of owning a faster and more practically constructed vessel. The locals were slow to concede, but when one or two were persuaded and Archer began producing boats that took prizes in local regattas, other clients began coming to his new slipways and sheds at Tolderodden.

By the turn of the century, Colin Archer's pilot boats were legendary worldwide. He had long since married and moved to a smaller house he had built at Tolderodden. He had been elected a member of the Institution of Naval Architects in London—an honor for a foreigner. The king of Norway conferred on him the Cross of the Order of St. Olaf, and he received the silver medal of the Royal Geographic Society.

A decade later, his assistant, longtime friend, and draftsman, Axel Harman, died. Archer, nearing 80, decided to retire. He spent his final years writing to his many friends and advising anyone who was interested in the advantages of owning and sailing a Colin Archer design. For his work on the pilot and rescue boats (he was district foreman of the rescue society), he was presented with a special diploma recognizing his enormous contribution to safety at sea. Just as John Alden was sowing the seeds of foundation in yacht design, Colin Archer died at the age of 89 in 1921. His legacy to the yachting industry was enormous, a veritable gold mine of sound architectural principles and common sense based on a lifetime of working experience gleaned from watching the building and working of his own inimitable designs.

In Colin Archer's lifetime, yachting, as it had come to be practiced in other parts of Europe, England, and the United States, barely existed in a similar format in Scandinavia. There was neither the money nor the time. But this did not discourage Archer either from participating in or encouraging the formation of a "yachting" society.

Several regattas were held around the coast during the summer months, and while most of the participants were fisherfolk, pilots, and rescue boats of the newly formed coastal rescue patrol service, observers noted with some surprise the speed of the entries sailed by Colin Archer. The designer was an avid pleasure boat sailor, and his command of the English language enabled him both to study articles published in the yachting press in England and to write his opinions for the same. He wrote extensively for *The Field,* elaborating on his own designs for the Redningskoites— sailing and motor rescue boats—of which many were eventually built.

These rescue boats were still being built in the early 1940s, long after their designer had died. Subsequently, many were sold into private ownership and were converted for cruising, a task for which they are admirably suited.

Why? Archer's boats were designed with these simple requirements in mind. Speed for the sake of it was unimportant, but a pilot or rescue boat had to have the ability to make to windward in the most atrocious conditions. If hove-to, it would be hove-to comfortably without need to call for assistance. Virtually all of his designs exploited the attributes of built-in buoyancy afforded by a particular hull design; hence the entry was fine but supported considerable flare, which was often carried through to the midships sections. These boats had a long, straight keel joined to a raking sternpost that curved forward in the upper sections and supported a distinctive tucked-in end that gave additional buoyancy in a following sea. The rudder stock ran the full length of the sternpost, the curved blade being controlled by a massive tiller instead of a wheel. Colin Archer maintained that the tiller allowed more feel to be transmitted to the helmsman and thus greater control in conditions likely to cause a broach or a knockdown.

One outstanding feature of these craft is their enormous beam and relatively shallow draft. On average, boats would be designed to reach an overall length of between 30 and 40 feet. The beam could be as much as 17 or 18 feet, which in the larger of the type gives a ratio of 2.35:1. The reputation of the Redningskoites spread far and wide, and Archer received many commissions to design similar craft for other countries, including Russia.

Design work was by no means confined to working craft. Archer received a number of commissions for cruising yachts from clients at home and farther afield. Looking at the collection of remaining designs it is clear that while Colin Archer avidly purveyed the attributes of his working craft, he was not slow to adapt features of yachts produced in other countries to his own design.

Long, drawn-out counters and even the odd clipper bow can be found among the more conventional double-ended variety for which he gained most of his fame. These yachts are not unattractive, but most are certainly hybrids of doubtful pedigree. One notable exception to this general rule is *Asgard,* a gaff-rigged ketch, 50 feet in length, designed and built for Erskine Childers, author of that recently reissued work, *The Riddle of the Sands.*

Asgard achieved certain notoriety in the hands of her owner. She was built in 1905 and used for extensive cruising until her owner used the yacht for gunrunning. He was an Irish patriot sympathetic to the Irish independence movement, and his activities ultimately led to his death: he was shot by firing squad in 1922.

Accounts of the exploits and sometimes hair-raising ad-ventures of many Archer-designed and -built "skoite"-type boats filtered out of Scandinavia in the postwar years. Encouraged by the tales told in *The Cruise of the Dream Ship,* by Ralph Stock, who sailed a 47-foot Archer-designed cutter, the *Oeger,* halfway around the world after World War I, yachtsmen in Britain began placing orders for similar craft with Norwegian yards. William Nutting, editor of an American motorboating magazine, had visited the Baltic in 1915 and been so impressed with the design of the Archer double-ender that he commissioned a rising young designer by the name of William Atkin to produce a set of lines for a 32 footer.

Nutting eventually had the boat built in Norway, where costs were considerably lower, but this was not before Atkin's drawings had been published in America. They aroused great interest from cruising yachtsmen, and three boats, named *Faith, Hope,* and *Charity,* were subsequently built to Atkin's design for his partner Henry Bixby. The yachts were given different names when they were sold, but their building, Nutting's access to the columns of yachting journals of the day, and his close association with William Atkin did much to cement the interest in Archer designs in America.

In 1925, William Nutting disappeared while on passage from Bergen to America in his *Leive Eiriksson,* but Atkin continued to produce designs for double-enders and at one stage managed to interest John Alden in the concept. Although not a double-ender, an Alden schooner called *Saracen* (ex *Kinkajou*), built in 1924, bears certain similarities to some of Archer's yacht designs. A slightly snubbed bow with fine entry and more than an average amount of freeboard leads aft to a high tucked-in counter. She was a long-keeled short-ended type, designed primarily for rugged offshore work in the North Atlantic.

Of the original three Archer types designed by Atkin, *Charity* became *Eric* and ultimately the most popular Atkin double-ender. Many were produced over a period of five decades or more. William Garden, a Victoria, British Columbia, designer world famous for his cruising and motor yachts, produced the 30-foot *Bull Frog* ketch rigged cruiser in 1972. Based on the lines of an earlier yacht of the same name, *Bull Frog* was not far removed from Colin Archer's original lines. A decade earlier, Garden had produced the plans for *Seal,* a 37-foot Archer-type that he described as a "sturdy, seaworthy and pleasant little ship under sail."

In recent years, a revival of interest in Colin Archer types has spread from Scandinavia; in Sweden and Norway, a Colin Archer Club exists soley for the purpose of promoting Archer's work and designs and building exact replicas in glass-reinforced plastics. In America, the Westsail Corporation took one of William Atkin's 32-foot double-ended designs and revamped it for mass production.

In Bermuda, Paul Erling Johnson, designer, boatbuilder, writer, and artist—not to mention seaman and long-distance voyager—is probably more familiar with Archer's work than any other designer. Born on the Hamble River aboard a converted Redningskoite called *Escape* (his parents still live on it), Paul Johnson sailed to America and the Caribbean in a converted Shetland fishing smack in the early sixties. He later purchased a church made of matured pitch pine and from it built his first "Archer" cruiser. When Venus Yachts was established on Bermuda, Johnson built two identical 42 footers with colossal beam and called them *Venus* and *Moon*. The latter belongs to friends; *Venus* is Johnson's voyaging home and floating advertisement.

Constructed of grp (glass-reinforced plastic) using the Airex foam sandwich technique, *Venus* has since spawned innumerable offspring, built in timber and grp, along the eastern seaboard of the United States and in the West Indies. I have watched *Venus* trounce a fleet of heavy gaff-rigged veterans in annual gaffers races in England, and Johnson has many trophies attesting to the design's seaworthiness and speed. *Venus, Moon,* and many other Johnson-designed and -built double-enders are frequently entered in regattas in Antigua and are just as likely to turn up in other far-flung corners of the earth having traveled thousands of miles through gales and doldrums without so much as a whimper.

In many respects, Johnson is the archetypal Archer. The latter made nearly all of his drawings on squared graph paper, a most unusual technique for a naval architect. Paul Johnson has acquired the habits of Alden and the techniques of Archer, producing endless piles of paper depicting modifications to the ideal. But he will not sit for long and ruminate on the pros and cons. He would sooner be off and sailing, demonstrating to nonbelievers who might care to sit huddled in an oilskin, the thrills of sailing such a heavy beast in a gale of wind. Many who have done so have needed no further persuasion when it came to signing on the dotted line.

Johnson's Venus *heels to a gale of wind during an annual Solent outing for old gaffers. The 42-foot yacht is home to Johnson as he sails to and from exotic ports to design and build yachts for others.*

CHAPTER 5

A Quantum Leap

In his 1746 thesis *Traite du Navire*, Pierre Bouguer wrote, "Experience would be the best means of perfecting naval architecture, if it were possible; but it is plain enough that practice is insufficient in many cases. It is certain that if this alone is capable of perfecting some parts, it has need, in an infinity of others, to be aided by the light of theory."

The "light of theory" was slow in having any marked effect on yacht racing for well over a hundred years. International yacht racing, such as it was, was confined more or less entirely to those spectacles of wealth staged off the city of New York. The America's Cup was a battlefield shared by the stinking rich of the East Coast of America and the well-heeled patrons from English aristocracy who—because of a patently one-sided set of rules laid down in the Deed of Gift—were required to sail their challengers to the venue by way of the North Atlantic.

Wind and sea conditions on the American East Coast differed radically from those in Europe. The open-sea crossing of more than 3,000 miles had a somewhat sobering effect on English designers attempting to produce a challenger with winning potential. In the 1870s and 1880s these European goliaths of yachting tended to be overweight and undercanvased, the lead mine versus the skimming dish. The British allowed that the Yanks were "faster" but less seaworthy, not that that mattered much when it came to racing; the Americans still won and would continue to dominate the arena for decades.

Left: *Replica of the schooner America at rest off Cowes in 1968.* Above: *The America's Cup, the silver claret jug handed to America's owners in 1851.*

British boats sailed the Atlantic fitted out in the same way in which they left the launching ways—full of heavy Victorian furniture, carpets, potted ferns, and heaven knows what home-away-from-home comforts their owners could not bear to do without. Members of the contemporary British aristocracy sailed in the manner to which they were accustomed to living ashore, and little attention was given to the subtler ways of trying to make a yacht go faster. Hence, the bottoms of challengers spawned weeds and barnacles on planks that were rough hewn and occasionally grain swollen.

Blinded by the prospect of retrieving an ornate and singularly unattractive Victorian silver pitcher, owners paid designers handsomely for beautiful yachts that would have been better suited to world cruising than to match racing, so the defenders and challengers were closely matched only rarely. This state of play had lasted for a very long time.

The America's Cup is the oldest international sporting trophy of its kind. The Royal Yacht Squadron had planned a series of races off Cowes to celebrate the Great Exhibition of 1851, and at the invitation of its commodore, the Earl of Wilton, the New York Yacht Club sent the schooner *America* across the Atlantic. On the way to Cowes she met the British yacht *Laverock*, which had sailed out to meet her. On the run back to the island, the British boat was soundly beaten.

In those days, there was no handicapping as such. Wagers on the side were always considerable, but on this occasion the British were somewhat wary of the Yankee, which was obviously out to show its host what racing was all about.

At 1000 hours sharp on August 22, 1851, eighteen yachts raised anchor on sighting the starting signal and set sail to the eastward on a course that would lead them 53 miles around the Isle of Wight and back to the finishing line off the Royal Yacht Squadron. The solitary American schooner was racing seventeen British yachts that varied in size from the 47 tons of the favorite, *Aurora*, to the 392-ton, three-masted schooner *Brilliant*. The prize was the Hundred Guinea Cup presented by the Royal Yacht Squadron.

A moderate southwesterly blew for most of the day as the fleet ran down the Solent, past the *Victoria and Albert*, on which Queen Victoria was embarked, toward the Nab lightship. On the homeward leg, *America* was only 8 miles ahead of the *Aurora* when she had reached the Needles. The two, now miles ahead of the rest of the fleet, reached up the western Solent against a foul tide and a dying wind, the little British yacht bravely trying to close the gap. At the finish at about 8:30 P.M., *America* was the leader by 18 minutes.

Thistle, *designed by George Lennox Watson for the James Bell syndicate of 1887.*

THE RACE AROUND THE ISLE OF WIGHT, AUGUST 22, 1851

YACHT	TONNAGE	RIG	OWNER
BEATRICE	161	Schooner	Sir W. P. Carew
VOLANTE	48	Cutter	Mr. J. L. Craigie
ARROW	84	Cutter	Mr. T. Chamberlayne
WYVERN	205	Schooner	Duke of Marlborough
IONE	75	Cutter	Mr. Almon Hill
CONSTANCE	218	Schooner	Marquis of Conyngham
TITANIA	100	Schooner	Mr. R. Stephenson
GIPSY QUEEN	160	Schooner	Sir H. P. Hoghton
ALARM	193	Cutter	Mr. J. Weld
MONA	82	Cutter	Lord Alfred Paget
BRILLIANT	393	Barque	Mr. G. Holland Ackers
AMERICA	200	Schooner	Mr. J. C. Stevens
BACCHANTE	80	Cutter	Mr. B. H. Jones
FREAK	60	Cutter	Mr. Wm. Curling
STELLA	65	Cutter	Mr. R. Frankland
ECLIPSE	50	Cutter	Mr. H. S. Fearon
FERNANDE	127	Cutter	Major M. Martyn
AURORA	47	Cutter	Mr. Le Marchant Thomas

Had the New York Yacht Club sent a vessel of another name to Cowes that year, the America's Cup might not have existed to this day. Had there been a handicapping system, *Aurora* would have beaten the larger competitor by a wide margin. The race began at 1000 hours in a light breeze of westerly wind. *Titania, Stella,* and *Fernande* did not start. It was reported at the time that the schooner *America* was wearing the finest suit of sails yet seen in British waters.

The finishing times were as follows:

America	2037 hrs 22nd
Aurora	2055 hrs 22nd
Bacchante	2130 hrs 22nd
Eclipse	2145 hrs 22nd

The barque *Brilliant* finished at 0120 hours on August 23. She was a square-rigged vessel and still managed to beat all of the British schooners entered. The *Arrow* went aground near Ventnor. The *Alarm* went to her assistance along with several other entrants and therefore lost time. Off St. Lawrence, the bowsprit of the *Volante* was carried away by the *Freak*. There was, however, little doubt in the minds of observers that *America* was faster than the bulk of the fleet.

Built in New York on Twelfth Street and launched in May 1851, *America* was designed by George Steers and William H. Brown. She had been bought by a syndicate headed by John C. Stevens that included his brother and four other members of the NYYC. The schooner yacht's dimensions were as follows: length overall, 101 feet 9 inches; waterline length, 90 feet 3 inches; beam, 22 feet 6 inches; draft, 11 feet 6 inches; and measurement tonnage 170. She carried a sail area of 5,263 square feet.

Six years after the cup had been won, the surviving members of the *America* syndicate gave their prize to the New York Yacht Club on the understanding that any foreign yacht club be allowed to make a challenge for it. The conditions for custodianship and challenges for the cup were contained in an elaborate Deed of Gift. New races did not commence again until 1870, when the original winner, *America*, by then the property of the United States Naval Academy, took part in the first cup regatta. She came home fourth, but the British, who had entered James Ashbury's *Cambria*, were tenth.

If longevity could be measured by time alone for the purpose of this work, then the schooner yacht *America* would surely head the list. After the 1870 races, the yacht was refitted and was used as a training vessel until, 90 years later, she had deteriorated so badly that she was partly demolished when the shed into which she was being hauled for slipping collapsed.

From 1870 until 1890, America's Cup racing continued in much the same lopsided vein. Challenging yachts came and were defeated. There were no constraints on appearances. A yacht was a yacht in the traditional sense of the word: a palatial floating home for its owners and guests. Apart from the removal of a few loose trappings, such as plants and carpets, no one saw the need or necessity to adopt what we would call today a more professional attitude. There was no precedent. Yachting was very much a leisurely activity pursued in a manner to which the gentry of the day wished to remain accustomed.

Enter the genius, "the Wizard of Bristol"—Nathaniel Green Herreshoff, known as Captain Nat. Naval architect, shipbuilder, and marine engineer, he was brother of James Brown Herreshoff and a partner in Herreshoff Manufacturing Company. From the 1890s until 1924, he was America's leading yacht designer.

He formed Herreshoff Manufacturing in 1878 with brother John managing the finance and construction schedules. Nathaniel looked after designing, engineering, and ideas. The partnership thrived. They were among the first yacht builders to build upside-down over molds using double skins on frames stitched together with iron floors and knees. *Gloriana* in 1891, *Reliance*, and the America's Cup defenders *Vigilant*, *Defender*, and *Columbia* were just a handful of the many great yachts drawn and built by this dedicated team.

Nat Herreshoff was the product of a burgeoning America, a new country in which progress in manufacturing was being made faster than in any other country since the industrial revolution. He was better noted for his engineering ideas than for yacht designing, though the latter is ultimately what made him famous.

During a period when American ship designers were pursuing speed for the sake of it rather than for financial returns, Nathaniel Herreshoff was busy producing steam-driven launches that would enable the more wealthy residents of Long Island to flit across the Sound at breakneck speeds and arrive exhilarated and in time for a good day's work in the prosperous and fast-rising city of Manhattan.

Herreshoff was born in Bristol, Rhode Island, and was 42 when he designed *Gloriana*, the first real racing yacht to differ radically from her many predecessors. *Gloriana* was 70 feet overall with a waterline length of 45 feet 4 inches on a beam of 12 feet 7 inches. She carried 4,137 square feet of sail on a 10-foot draft and was a great success in the 46-foot class, in which she raced under the length and sail area rule. She was not the first yacht with a fin keel (E. H. Bentall produced *Evolution* in 1880, unsuccessful due to her extreme narrowness of beam, only 6 feet 6 inches on a 51-foot waterline), but her short waterline length and huge sail area, long overhanging bow, and counter became a winning formula. George Lennox Watson's earlier *Thistle* was probably Herreshoff's starting point, and Watson followed *Gloriana* with *Britannia*, which raced under three different rating rules during her 40-year career.

It seemed that with one stroke Herreshoff was able to do for racing what many had puzzled over for decades. Where speed was the prime requisite, straight stems and long keels were abolished. *Gloriana* epitomized a "quantum leap" in yacht design. From then on, yachts proceeded upwind at speeds unseen or unheard of in previous decades. Yacht racing demanded new ideas from naval architects to maximize the speed potential; a fin keel and long overhangs were simply not enough in themselves to beat the competition.

Herreshoff concentrated on refining these ideas by designing lighter yachts. He was well aware of the problems caused by fouling and rough-sawn planks. Less resistance and a decreased displacement with increased stability must produce a faster hull. Get rid of the heavy wooden deck and the steel deck frames, remove the trappings of inner comfort, improve the efficiency of blocks and tackle by making these important but sundry items lighter, cram on more sail—and speed would increase.

In 1895, Herreshoff designed *Defender* for an America's Cup defense syndicate. The syndicate manager, Oliver Iselin, went to France to look over a yacht called *Vendenesse*, the hull of which was plated with aluminium. Electrolysis was already eating the hull away, but Herreshoff listened intently as Iselin reported his findings. *Defender* was built.

She was 123 feet overall with a waterline length of 88 feet 5 inches. *Defender* had a draft of almost 20 feet and carried a crew of 64, nearly six times the number carried by present-day 12-meter America's Cup yachts. Her hull below the waterline was built of bronze plate; her topsides and deck, aluminium. Lord Dunraven's *Valkyrie III*, that year's challenger, was heavier and six feet longer, and during the ensuing duel in New York Harbor, where some 200 spectator craft had gathered to watch the fight, Dunraven lost his cool. *Defender's* crew, he said, had shifted her ballast while the yacht was being cleaned and prepared for the regatta. She should have been remeasured. Dunraven sailed away in disgust and then accused the New York Yacht Club of fraud. There was uproar. Dunraven was relieved of his honorary membership of the NYYC, and another end of an era was logged in America's Cup history. No true blooded aristocrats would challenge for the cup again.

Some say that *Defender* was the most expensive battery ever built. Beautiful she was not, at least not out of her

Right: *Deck laying on* Shamrock V *required at least 16 men, overseen by the gentleman at right with hands in pocket and trilby hat.* Below: *Pouring 90 tons of hot lead to make the ballast keel of the Nicholson-designed* Velsheda *at the Gosport boatyard.*

element. She was the first of the monster yachts, but by no means the biggest. That honor belongs to *Reliance*.

Reliance was possibly the largest sloop ever built. Herreshoff refined *Defender's* lines in a half-model whittled in just a few days. (Making models was a Herreshoff pleasure. When finished, the feel of the model would tell the genius what, if anything, was wrong. He was hardly ever wrong.) *Reliance* measured 143 feet 8 inches overall and was one foot longer on the waterline than *Defender*—the new yacht's overhangs were truly massive. Her draft was almost the same as *Defender's*, and she spread some 16,159.45 square feet of sail on a 25-foot 10-inch beam. Charlie Barr skippered the yacht, as he had done for the syndicate's three previous defenders.

Above: Resolute *in dry dock at Bath Iron Works, Maine.* Left: *The new framework of the J class* Endeavour *during restoration in England. Pictured is the new owner, Elizabeth Meyer.* Opposite: *The Francis Herreshoff-designed J class* Whirlwind, *one of the prettiest of her type ever built.*

Herreshoff's own manufacturing corporation built *Reliance* out of steel. The topside plates were said to be half as thick as those of a modern 12 meter. Everything about the yacht was big, bigger than ever before, and one can see why by looking at the huge cloud of sail she was designed to carry. Her rig towered 200 feet. The mainsheet alone was 1,000 feet long. Her spinnaker pole was nearly 84 feet in length, and all the strength of a dozen men would have been required to move it.

Such rigs were positively dangerous. This was a period when racing yacht design produced yachts with more sail crammed onto a single mast than had ever been seen before. *Reliance* had been logged at over 17 knots, but no one knew how much faster she would go or in what extreme conditions she could be sailed. No one was prepared to take the risk. Then, as now, with so much money invested in the building of the ultimate racing machine, syndicates and race organizers agreed an upper limit on the conditions under which racing could take place. For this reason, America's Cup defenders at this time were of comparatively lighter build than their European counterparts, which, because of a condition of the Deed of Gift, were forced to sail to the race across an unpredictable ocean.

This harnessing of wind power became an engineer's nightmare, for few of these machines could be sailed in anything but sheltered waters without fear of the whole rig being torn from its step. Herreshoff was by now aware that yachts like *Reliance* could not continue to be built if further progress were to be made. He had been hard at work for several years devising a new rule that would soon ring the death knell for these monster machines.

Reliance lived for a little over nine months. She was scrapped in the same year she won the cup. Built at a cost of some $450,000, she was the last great racing sloop. Her gear was saved and kept in store, some of it to resurface years later and be put to good use. In the meantime, a war in Europe loomed on the horizon. Thomas Lipton's *Shamrock IV,* a Charles Nicholson-designed rule-breaker, arrived in New York as hostilities commenced. Put on mothballs, the challenger was not to emerge again for six years, and when she finally did, Herreshoff's *Resolute* was there to beat her.

The Burgess-Stephens-designed J class yacht Ranger, *the biggest and best of her class.*

The Universal Rule had actually been in force in America for two years before *Reliance* slid down the ways. This rule was essentially the product of Herreshoff's unstinting research, but it was to be another five years before it became accepted in Europe. The new rule favored heavier-built yachts constructed to Lloyd's scantling rules.

Lipton had also been campaigning for years to have the Deed of Gift changed, and in 1927 the J class of the Universal Rule was adopted for America's Cup contenders. Now came the turn of Starling Burgess.

The Js were and, for those few that remain, are the most fascinating of yacht racing machines. Not as big as their earlier predecessors, but still massive, the class measured some 75 to 85 feet on the waterline and 120 feet overall. These yachts were stripped-out shells; pure thoroughbreds, immensely expensive day racing keelboats built and sailed by American millionaires in competition with their English counterparts.

The defending yachts of 1930, 1934, and 1937, *Enterprise*, *Rainbow*, and *Ranger*, were all designed by Burgess for owner and skipper Harold Vanderbilt, member of the wealthy railroad-building family. Nathaniel Herreshoff had been succeeded by his son Francis, who in 1929 designed *Whirlwind*, arguably one of the prettiest American J class yachts ever conceived.

She was the last of the four defender candidates built for the 1930 event, and because of a lack of skilled platers was constructed composite, in the same fashion as Watson's *Britannia*. She had an unusually wide after deck, in keeping perhaps with her owner George Pynchon's tentative ideas to convert her for cruising should she not be selected as the defender. She was a Bermudan cutter, the first J with a double headsail, a feature that was immediately copied by successive yachts. *Whirlwind*'s lead ballast keel was contained inside a bronze casting that could not possibly rot. The hull and deck were braced throughout with a series of steel straps. There were many innovative ideas in *Whirlwind*, but she was not ultimately selected to defend the cup, a task admirably carried out by *Enterprise*.

Despite relegation, *Whirlwind* must stand with other, more successful names of her class, for it was her rig, copied and modified by others, that improved the class and produced efficient racing machines, albeit with painful slowness. Nicholson's "Marconi" rig, the triangular main instead of the gaff of the previous 50 years, was recognizably more efficient in all conditions, and that of *Whirlwind* was actually more advanced than many realized at the time. Not only did her designer attempt to go from a three headsail rig to a two, but by introducing a midstay such as was then in use on smaller 6-meter craft, the size of the staysail was so small as to be insignificant in certain conditions. *Whirlwind* could have had a single headsail.

Designers were still unraveling the problems of the rig at this stage. It was far from trustworthy; several years were to pass before its idiosyncrasies became more understandable. In 1935, B. Heckstall-Smith described the Bermudan

rig as new—*five* years after it had first been introduced on *Whirlwind!* In September of the same year, he was to write in *Yachting World:* "It is a costly and unkindly rig with which to sail bold 'Channel Races' in strong breezes. In such weather it is very effective, but if breakage occurs [as it had done that season with Sopwith's *Endeavour* and the American *Yankee*], it is likely to be a serious one."

One can see how designers of the time approached their respective commissions. On the one hand, it was thought that *Endeavour* should have been more strongly rigged for the often heavy airs of the Channel in spite of the fact that she was conceived as a challenger for the America's Cup, where one might expect to experience a sometimes sloppy ground swell and moderate winds. Herreshoff, Jr., designed *Whirlwind* for just those conditions, while Nicholson produced *Endeavour* bearing in mind both conditions off Newport and a lengthy transatlantic voyage. Her rig, however, was better suited to eastern seaboard sailing than forays into the English Channel, where steep, choppy seas and a gale of wind could wreak havoc in about as much time as it takes to snap one's fingers.

Of all the J boats of the 1930s, T.O.M. Sopwith's first *Endeavour* is certainly one of the world's outstanding sailing yachts. I say "is," because unlike many of her near sisterships long since scrapped, *Endeavour I* lives, having undergone a complete restoration at huge expense in the ownership of Elizabeth Meyer.

She was a Nicholson protégé designed to win the "auld mug" back for Britain. She almost succeeded, taking the first two races from the American Burgess-designed *Rainbow*. Sopwith would have won the third race had he covered his opponent properly and had not the Yankee owner gone below for a nap while his second in command, Sherman Hoyt, took the wheel. It was Hoyt's bluff that won the day.

At the time, observers felt that the British yacht had an edge in speed that the Yankee lacked, even though the Yankee won the next three races (one through disqualification). When it was all over, Charles Nicholson agreed to swap *Endeavour*'s plans with Burgess in exchange for *Rainbow*'s. He need not have bothered, for the successful defender hardly told Nicholson anything he did not already know. What Nicholson knew only too well was that had *Endeavour* been properly crewed with the professionals she had tuned and trained with since her launching, she could very well have beaten the Yankee.

The late Jeff Gilby, who worked the topsail sheets on *Endeavour*, once recalled how, shortly before the yacht was

Opposite top: Endeavour *being launched from the builder's yard of Camper & Nicholson.* Opposite bottom: Endeavour, *her hull completely rebuilt, ready for relaunching in 1986.*

due to sail for America, a dispute arose between the professional crew and the owner, T.O.M. Sopwith.

The great yacht had five jib topsails with strain gauges on deck so that the crew could keep an eye on overloading. Training invariably took place in mid Channel against the trials horse *Velsheda*. They once gybed the spinnaker 17 times while Lady Sopwith stood by with a stopwatch.

Gilby's basic weekly wage was £2.75 with an extra 13 pence thrown in because he also acted as signalman. Out of this he had to buy his own food. The rest of the crew were equally worried lest they would lose money while abroad by having to pay for the upkeep of their homes in England. The crew had been promised an extra pound for the first race of the America's Cup, fifteen shillings for the second race, and ten shillings for the third.

The crew members were unhappy about this arrangement and proposed to the owner that they would go to the States only if they could make a similar deal as that made by the owner of *Shamrock* and his crew. Lipton had offered his crew a substantial bonus as an incentive to get the crew psyched into a winning mood.

Endeavour's crew met with Sopwith on deck. He refused their proposal, whereupon the whole crew walked off and found berths on racers intending to stay in home waters for the season. Sopwith cobbled together a scratch crew of amateurs recruited by the Royal Corinthian Yacht Club at Burnham on Crouch and set sail for America shortly after.

Endeavour I measured 130 feet overall, 83 feet on the waterline, and was constructed from riveted steel plate on 74 ring frames. She was a centerboarder, so when her plate was dropped she had an effective draft of 24 feet. She carried 80 tons of ballast and displaced approximately 165 tons.

She was built by Nicholson's own firm, Camper & Nicholson, at their Gosport yard in Portsmouth Harbor. In 1935, a year after she had lost to *Rainbow,* she raced against seven other "first-class" yachts, including *Westward,* the J class *Velsheda* and *Yankee, Britannia, Candida, Shamrock,* and *Astra.* In 35 starts that year, *Endeavour* had 12 wins, 10 seconds, and 6 thirds—28 top positions. There wasn't much doubt in the mind of her designer about her speed. She was probably just the teeniest bit on the heavy side for the conditions off Newport.

Nicholson's *Endeavour II,* which measured 87 feet on the waterline, was less successful in 1937, but by that time yacht designing was no longer a seat-of-the-pants affair. Burgess was using models in tank tests in earnest, and he had been joined by a younger man, at Vanderbilt's insistence.

Aerial view of Cambria, *the unsuccessful challenger for the America's Cup of 1870. Now fully restored,* Cambria *is cruising as a ketch.*

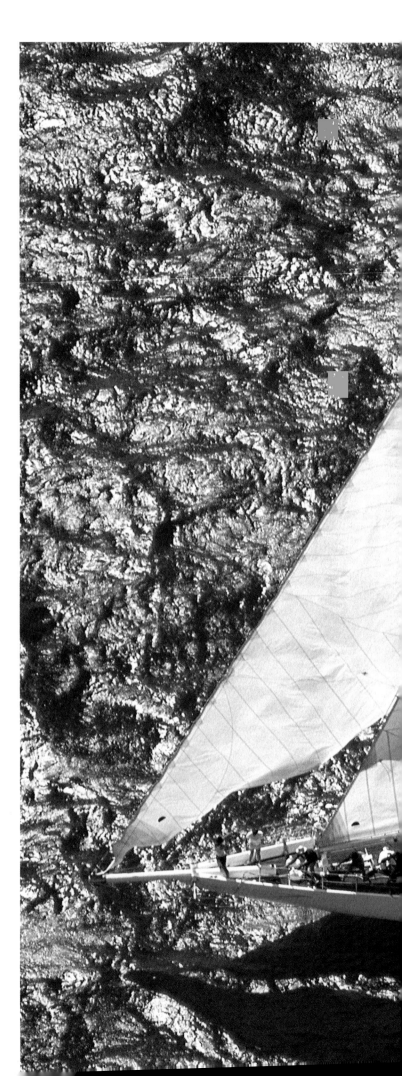

due to sail for America, a dispute arose between the professional crew and the owner, T.O.M. Sopwith.

The great yacht had five jib topsails with strain gauges on deck so that the crew could keep an eye on overloading. Training invariably took place in mid Channel against the trials horse *Velsheda*. They once gybed the spinnaker 17 times while Lady Sopwith stood by with a stopwatch.

Gilby's basic weekly wage was £2.75 with an extra 13 pence thrown in because he also acted as signalman. Out of this he had to buy his own food. The rest of the crew were equally worried lest they would lose money while abroad by having to pay for the upkeep of their homes in England. The crew had been promised an extra pound for the first race of the America's Cup, fifteen shillings for the second race, and ten shillings for the third.

The crew members were unhappy about this arrangement and proposed to the owner that they would go to the States only if they could make a similar deal as that made by the owner of *Shamrock* and his crew. Lipton had offered his crew a substantial bonus as an incentive to get the crew psyched into a winning mood.

Endeavour's crew met with Sopwith on deck. He refused their proposal, whereupon the whole crew walked off and found berths on racers intending to stay in home waters for the season. Sopwith cobbled together a scratch crew of amateurs recruited by the Royal Corinthian Yacht Club at Burnham on Crouch and set sail for America shortly after.

Endeavour I measured 130 feet overall, 83 feet on the waterline, and was constructed from riveted steel plate on 74 ring frames. She was a centerboarder, so when her plate was dropped she had an effective draft of 24 feet. She carried 80 tons of ballast and displaced approximately 165 tons.

She was built by Nicholson's own firm, Camper & Nicholson, at their Gosport yard in Portsmouth Harbor. In 1935, a year after she had lost to *Rainbow*, she raced against seven other "first-class" yachts, including *Westward*, the J class *Velsheda* and *Yankee*, *Britannia*, *Candida*, *Shamrock*, and *Astra*. In 35 starts that year, *Endeavour* had 12 wins, 10 seconds, and 6 thirds—28 top positions. There wasn't much doubt in the mind of her designer about her speed. She was probably just the teeniest bit on the heavy side for the conditions off Newport.

Nicholson's *Endeavour II*, which measured 87 feet on the waterline, was less successful in 1937, but by that time yacht designing was no longer a seat-of-the-pants affair. Burgess was using models in tank tests in earnest, and he had been joined by a younger man, at Vanderbilt's insistence.

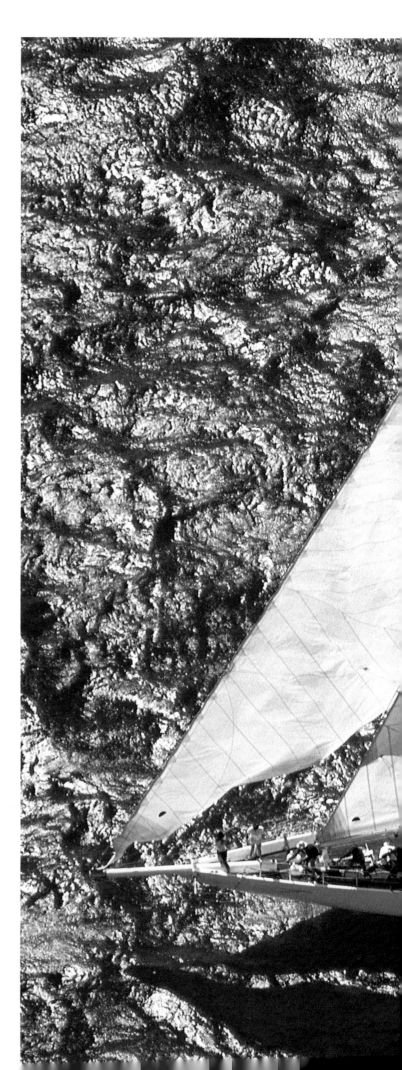

Aerial view of Cambria, *the unsuccessful challenger for the America's Cup of 1870. Now fully restored,* Cambria *is cruising as a ketch.*

CHAPTER 6

Summers of Success

The historical horizon of yachting is peppered with jagged peaks. Looking back over one's shoulder to those distant summers, it is not easy to see this grand shimmering vista as anything but a mirage, and yet we are aware all the while that some extraordinary force has been at work, sculpting the horizon so that we may readily identify significant changes in shape and pattern. What is not so clear, despite the continuing statement, is the schooner *America's* involvement and how her success has affected almost every facet of yacht design to date.

America was the force. The grand event, the right and fight to defend and challenge for her prize, has been the vehicle that has carried the force through the minds of yacht designers ever since. Designers may have set out to solve specific problems unrelated to the America's Cup, but that event has spurred designers to radical departures from the norm. It has been and still is the catalyst of creativity in the designers' quest for an answer to the perennial problem of how to make a particular solid mass pass through fluid with the greatest of ease. So this force has become the thread that weaves and secures our grand vista into a huge tapestry.

Left: *The Nicholson-designed*
Velsheda, *fully restored and
sailing in the Solent in the
1980s.* Above: *The rebuilt 6M*
Nada *cruising in the Solent.*

Left *(left to right): Starling Burgess with Olin and Rod Stephens and Drake Sparkman at their Madison Avenue office discuss the design for a new America's Cup yacht,* Ranger, *in the 1930s. Opposite:* Dorade, *designed by Olin Stephens, was first in her class in the Bermuda Race in the year of her launch, then the Transatlantic Race and the Fastnet the following year.*

The smaller peaks represent those designers who have produced a norm, craft designed to perform a particular function in one facet of the market. Some of these craft may perform that function more elegantly and more efficiently than other, similar craft, but essentially they are spin-offs from the taller peaks, created by visionary draftsmen who have occasionally produced a benchmark that all others try to emulate. Tall, jagged peaks that appear close together indicate an era during which several designers produced exceptional craft. And so it goes on.

When Charles Nicholson's *Endeavour I* gave Vanderbilt cause to imagine that his head might replace the America's Cup in a glass case in the New York Yacht Club's trophy room in 1934, and after Hoyt had saved the day, Olin Stephens was already well established as a rising star in yacht design.

Olin and his brother Rod began their sailing careers at Cape Cod in the early 1920s, sailing out of Sandy Neck in an engineless knockabout called *Corker.* Their father managed the family business, the Stephens Fuel Company, originally founded by their grandfather in New York's Bronx. As summers progressed, the boys' father purchased larger craft. Soon they were expert sailors, and by 1925 both were sailing with Sherman Hoyt in 6 meters on Long Island Sound.

In 1926, after one term at MIT, Olin drew his first 6 meter. Rod had also tried university studies, but the subject matter was commerical, too far removed from the yachts he had grown to love. He left Cornell and joined his brother, applying Olin's draftsmanship and theory to practice. The two became a team.

The Larchmont Yacht Club had been hunting around for a new design for their younger club members. Assisted by Drake Sparkman, Olin's design for a junior class boat was swiftly built and accepted by the club. Sparkman became a partner, putting up the funds when necessary to keep the partnership afloat, but as 6 meters were much in demand in 1929 with a British/American regatta in the offing, there was little pessimism about the future. That year, the Sparkman & Stephens partnership received commissions for five new 6 meters and one 8 meter.

The partnership developed into a corporation. With the depression about to hit America, more cautious men might have held off. At Sparkman & Stephens, success bred success, and the 6 meters slid down the ways of Minneford's in New York and were raced with great success.

It was at this time too that Olin was already scheming to produce the most radical and most influential ocean racing yacht of her time. *Dorade* was launched 1930, when the Alden schooners prevailed. *Dorade* was Olin Stephens's

Opposite top: *The owner's cabin of* Freedom *features all the luxury one would expect in a vessel this size (135 feet l.o.a.). Designed by Sparkman & Stephens for William Simon, former secretary of the U.S. Treasury,* Freedom *was built of aluminum by Pichiotti's of Italy and was launched in the spring of 1986. Opposite bottom: The owner's den of* Freedom. *Above: Craftsmen at the Camper & Nicholson yard completely rebuilt the hull and rigging of* Shamrock V, *Lipton's last America's Cup challenger. The hull was stripped to its steel frames, which were rebuilt and then fitted with bright, new teak planks.*

reaction to the workboat ancestry of the Malabars. His creation was nothing like any of them. "I much preferred the narrower, deeper type with an efficient rig," Olin told Tim Jeffery in a feature article in *Yachting World* in 1981.

In her own way, *Dorade* was something of a hybrid. For an ocean racer, she was narrow, only 10 feet 3 inches on an overall length of 52 feet. She was also deep, having a draft of 8 feet. This configuration gave her a fine windward performance, a spin-off from the meter boats, which Olin had found would perform well offshore, given the right conditions.

On this hull, a Bermudan yawl rig was set to carry a relatively small amount of sail, only 1,100 square feet. Her relative lightness, however, gave the yacht great speed. It is said that *Dorade* had a tendency to roll heavily downwind during her early years until modifications were made to the main. After a season of runaway victories, S&S received a number of commissions for similar craft, and such was the success of these craft that the *Dorade* look continued to prevail for many years.

Her freeboard was high, partly to give extra height over the cabin sole and partly because the ends of the yacht were carried out to their natural conclusion. The design has what are called easy sections, which, while giving some buoyancy forward, would have made her quite wet in windward work. The bow profile, modified slightly in some other designs, runs in an elegant curve to the heel of the keel, so that if one were to arrange two profiles together, keels pointing outward, a near perfect arrowhead would be recognizable.

Minneford's was chosen to build the yacht, which was planked on steam-bent frames—another Stephens reaction to the heavy, sawn frames favored by Alden. But *Dorade* came out slightly heavier than her designer had wished. Her oak frames were on nine-inch centers; they probaby could have been spaced wider with no ill effect in her ultimate strength and a saving in weight.

Olin rebelled against the heavier and more conventional yacht designs then prevalent by incorporating his ideas on keelboat and meter yachts, but it was still widely felt at the time that inherent strength in a yacht could be achieved only by retaining mass; hence the large number of frames. Also, the "fin" keel, which had begun to emerge in the pre-war years with the great cup boats like *Reliance*, was not yet considered safe for offshore work, so keels were kept long and relatively deep, the rudder being hung on a raking after edge in much the same fashion as on most working craft.

At this time, the science of yacht design was still much in its infancy. Some work had been done on models with the foundation of the Stevens towing tank in Hoboken, New Jersey, by Professor Kenneth Davidson in the early thirties. But tank testing as we know it today was still pretty much a hit-and-miss affair. In the early years of his career, Olin Stephens worked closely with his brother Rod—the test pilot—and, like other designers, he was intuitive. Look now at other designs of the period, those, for example, of known fast working craft.

The Nova Scotia fishing schooners, more commonly referred to as Grand Banks schooners, were designed by W. J. Roue. *Bluenose* was probably the most famous and won races more or less continuously from the time of her launch in the early 1920s. The Gloucestermen could not beat her, even though they were lighter. Olin Stephens and his contemporaries would have looked to these working craft designs for the sheer pleasure of looking, but because of their intense interest they would have noted the many fine points of design, the formula that made such craft the success they were. The easy entry, buoyant sections in the ends and high bilge lines, the long keel and raked rudder— all of these points would have been noted by someone like Stephens and put to good use when occasion demanded.

In the year of her launch, *Dorade* was first in her class in the Bermuda Race. But for a navigational error, she might well have been first overall. The following year, she won the Transatlantic Race and her first Fastnet Race. She was up with the leaders again in the Bermuda Race of the following year, winning her class. Back in England in 1933, *Dorade* again won the Fastnet.

By now, the Stephens brothers were forging ahead. *Dorade* was followed by *Stormy Weather,* which returned to the Solent in 1935 by way of the Transatlantic Race, which she won. She also took victory in the Fastnet that year and then proceeded to thrash back to the States in a little more than 24 days, clipping two days off the previous record set by *Dorade.*

A quick glance at her lines would fool the uninitiated. Her profile is similar to that of *Dorade'*s, but that is all. *Stormy Weather* is a different kind of craft, the result of the wealth of experience gained in *Dorade* and the combination of other ideas.

Stormy Weather was nearly two feet longer overall with much the same increase in beam. Her draft, however, at 7 feet 11 inches, was less than *Dorade'*s, and she carried nearly 200 square feet more sail area. The sections are much more rounded from forward of amidships, leading aft. She has a tumblehome that would have given her an altogether drier and easier ride in a seaway. Her long, sweeping lines gave a high maximum speed, even in light airs. *Stormy Weather* displaced approximately 20 tons and, with the yawl rig much favored by many Americans at the time, was altogether a more stable, more seaworthy craft than *Dorade.*

Dorade was not outdated easily. While *Stormy Weather* was knocking up wins on one side of the world, *Dorade* went on to win the Honolulu race of 1936. In that same year Sopwith had made another challenge for the "auld mug," and Vanderbilt, worried that he might go through a repeat of the 1934 performance, commissioned Olin Stephens to work alongside Starling Burgess on the plans for a new defender.

By then a partner in the S&S firm, Rod Stephens was able

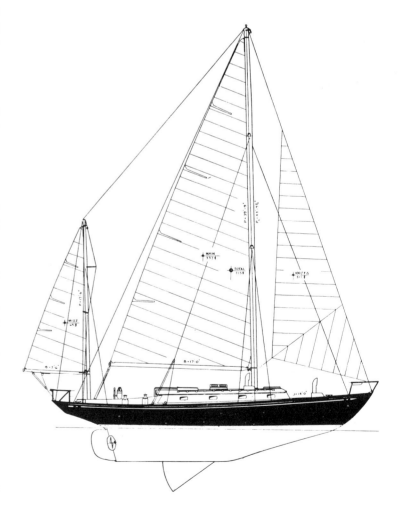

Below: *Plans of* Finisterre, *which measured 38 feet 7 inches overall and 27 feet 6 inches on the waterline with a beam of 11 feet 3 inches, which gave her capacious accommodation below decks.* Opposite: *Competing in the 635-mile Bermuda Race in the 1960s,* Finisterre *became the smallest yacht ever to win, with a corrected time of 64 hours.*

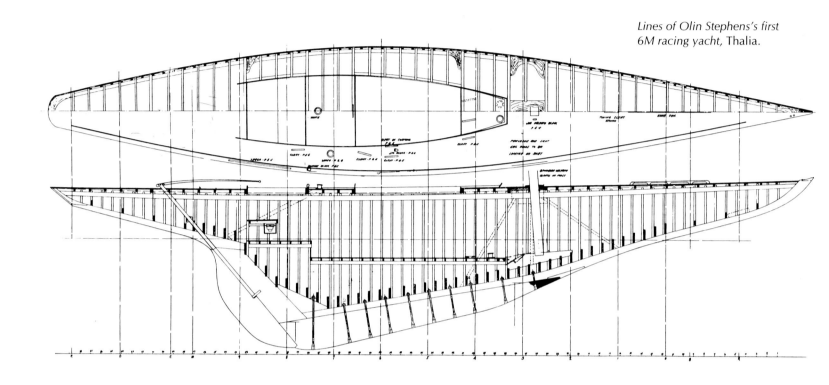

Lines of Olin Stephens's first 6M racing yacht, Thalia.

to keep an eye on the many new craft being built along the New England coast while model testing went apace in the Stevens tank. Charles Nicholson had swapped the plans of *Endeavour I* for a copy of those of *Rainbow.*

Olin Stephens was 28 years old; Burgess was his senior by 23 years. It was an unlikely combination, but the pair worked well together, testing models of their own against those of *Rainbow* and *Endeavour.* It was the first time a serious approach to tank testing had been made. Until then, models had been large—up to 20 feet long, in some instances—unwieldy, and, more importantly at the time, expensive. Professor Kenneth Davidson produced smaller, three-foot models that cost a lot less. The new models were very sophisticated, allowing measurements to be taken for angle of heel in a given wind situation as well as forward thrust.

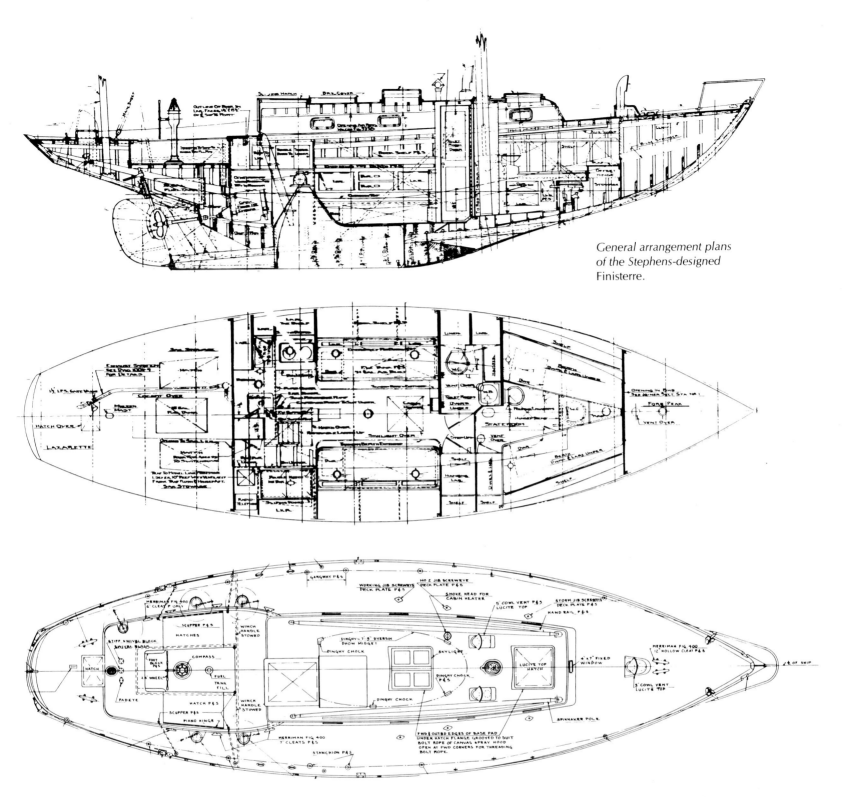

General arrangement plans of the Stephens-designed Finisterre.

The earlier J boats were tested over and over. There was pretty conclusive evidence to show that *Endeavour I* had indeed been faster than *Rainbow,* particularly on the wind. *Rainbow* was a better performer than *Weetamoe,* another candidate for the defense.

Burgess and Stephens had tank-tested four models. No. 77-C, which Stephens later admitted was to a Burgess design, was selected for the defense. Both designers worked on the lines to try and improve her appearance, for she had a rather ugly, bulbous bow and flattened stern, features that would later prove to be a major contribution to her speed.

Ranger, nicknamed the super J, was the largest of her class ever built. She was also to be the last. In her day, her snubbed-off nose caused much discussion, and certainly no one thought her beautiful. But as with *Britannia* in her day, looking at *Ranger* now leaves little doubt that she was indeed a state-of-the-art design—a magnificent, powerful ship with the lines of a greyhound.

She was 135 feet overall. Unlike previous defenders, *Ranger* was constructed entirely of steel with flush riveted plates at the Bath Iron Works in Maine. The company's president had offered to build the yacht at cost when it became clear that Vanderbilt would not find the necessary sponsorship among his contemporaries.

Ranger was launched in May 1937. Her mast, boom, and spinnaker poles were made of duralumin. She had bar rigging. Much of her deck furniture came from *Rainbow,* and her wardrobe of sails came from *Enterprise.* As trials progressed, it became clear that the new yacht was more powerful than any before her. New sails were made: 7,546 square feet of lightweight canvas. Her spinnaker covered an incredible 18,000 square feet. This great shark of a yacht went from speed to speed, and with her codesigner, Olin, and his brother Rod aboard in the afterguard, her performance seemed to be uncheckable.

By comparison, T.O.M. Sopwith's new challenger, *Endeavour II,* was a dog. When he saw the yacht out of the water for the first time, her designer, Charles Nicholson, said of *Ranger* that he thought she was the most revolutionary boat to emerge for fifty years. In the summer of 1937, the big new Yankee sailed in 34 races and won 32 of them by an average of a little over 7 minutes. In the final match with Nicholson's 136 footer, Vanderbilt swamped the British challenger by beating her in the first two races by 17 minutes and 18 minutes respectively. He could have continued and finished the event in the same style, but for the sake of history and sportsmanship, he chose to sail much closer matches in the last two races. The winning margins were down to 4 minutes.

By 1942, most of the racing Js were piles of scrap metal, on their way to becoming new parts for ships of a different kind: ocean greyhounds of war. Today, only a handful of these goliaths survive, and were it not for the determination of their respective owners, the few that are left would have long since disappeared beneath muddied creeks. Several times, *Velsheda* came close to following her predecessors to the knacker's yard. Now she sails under shortened rig, her riveted steel hull refurbished and her decks renewed. All of her original bird's-eye maple paneling was torn out long ago, before her present owner salvaged the hull and began a costly rebuilding program. *Endeavour I* might still be sitting in a huge cradle near Southampton were it not for John Amos and Elizabeth Meyer. Miss Meyer took over the restoration project, and a totally rebuilt legend slid back into the waters of the Solent in 1986. *Shamrock V* has been lovingly cared for and rebuilt, frame by frame, plank by plank. They are the last of these giants of sail, and with luck, when the new J class society has worked out a calender of events, many will be able to watch them sail again off the greens of Cowes and the shores of Newport.

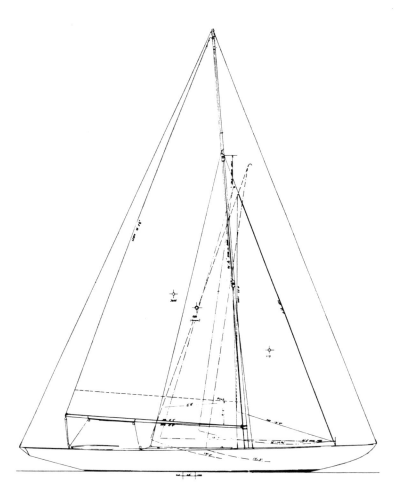

Below: *Sail plan of* Thalia. Opposite: Thalia. *Olin Stephens's first serious racing designs were concentrated on the 6M class;* Thalia *was his first.*

CHAPTER 7

The New Breed

If 1983 was the year in which the first radical changes in 12-meter design became historically significant, then 1986 must go on record as the year in which America's Cup challenging syndicate chiefs sailed completely off-course and gave all of their varied designers a virtual carte blanche to come up with something different.

"Different" is an inadequate description, for the twelves of the new breed were expected not only to follow in the successful mold of Ben Lexcen's 1983 cup winner, *Australia II,* by being fast *and* maneuverable, but were to be regarded by owners and competing syndicates as much a serious threat to one another as to any of the potential defenders.

Thirty-nine-year-old Johan Valentijn—designer for the *Freedom* syndicate in 1980, for Dennis Conner again in 1982–83 with *Magic* and *Liberty,* and designer of the 1986 Newport Beach, California, syndicate's *Eagle*—was encouraged to be more creative and to try whatever he liked, simply on the premise that because so many challenging syndicates would be involved, one or more would be bound to produce a boat that was even more radical in

Left: Lionheart *during her first sea trials under a gray Solent sky.* Above: A.J. Boyden's British challenger of 1980, Lionheart, *about to be launched.*

design than anything that had appeared since 12-meter match racing had begun in earnest in 1958. This seems to have been the course taken by many designers involved in the 1986–87 America's Cup event, but ultimately, and with the exception of two yachts, most of the twelves racing on the waters of Gage Roads off Fremantle were not so very different from Lexcen's 1983 winner. A "safe" marriage to convention within the parameters of the 12-Meter Rule while simultaneously exploring the varied potential of weird underwater appendages in the way of keels, skegs, fins, and wings seems to have been the order of the day.

While a number of syndicates cheerfully showed off the product of hundreds of hours of computer time and God knows what financial investment into design research, others were equally paranoid about keeping their various "weapons" under wraps. Perhaps they had good reason, for during the second and third rounds of both challengers' and defenders' elimination trials it became patently obvious that, almost without exception, those yachts with a weapon to hide were in the leading four. Those openly showing off had all but been eliminated from any further useful competition by observers and would no doubt have done themselves a huge favor by packing up and returning to the drawing board.

For the uninitiated, it will be of value here to discuss the antiquated rule that governs 12-meter construction and that, by the very nature of the beast, restricts match racing in twelves to one primary and one secondary sailing event: the America's Cup and the 12-Meter World Championship. In fairness to the reader interested only in the generality of yacht design and in particular to ocean greyhounds of more substance, or to fine cruisers capable of world-girdling voyages, it must be said that for all the hype applied to 12 meters, match racing over a lengthy course in relatively quiet waters is a most tiresome occupation for the spectator. These yachts are almost boringly slow, even in a stiff breeze. When the kind of winds come that would have most International Offshore Rule (IOR) boats piling on the canvas, the twelves are scudding for home lest anything break or be torn to irreparable shreds.

From the time the schooner *America* won the 1851 race staged over a course around the Isle of Wight until the turn of the century, there were almost as many rules as there were syndicates, owners, and clubs across the board of yacht racing. In 1907, an International Rule for various classes of yachts ranging in size from 10 to 25 meters (33 feet to 82 feet) was adopted. Over the years, the rule underwent various modifications, including one for the Olympics, but it was not until after World War II, by which time the J class had been melted, scrapped, or left to natural dereliction,

The British 12M Evaine of 1958 was used as a trial horse for the challenger Sceptre. Here she thrashes to windward at the start of the 1971 Fastnet Race. Note the long, thin counter.

that the New York Yacht Club and the Royal Yacht Squadron elected to adopt the rule for the America's Cup event, using the 12-meter class as the best alternative to those glamorous and expensive goliaths of the prewar years.

Other classes were rejected by the organizers of this event for various reasons, not least of which, one supposes, being that the twelves, when viewed from a respectable distance, could presume to be as glamorous and possibly as exciting to watch as their more magnificent forebears.

The twelves as a class were already in existence, the offspring of a rule aimed at encouraging inexpensive yacht racing for the less well off of 1906. By 1958, those innovative designers Rod and Olin Stephens had already done considerable work on improving the sailing qualities of twelves. Even before war broke out for the Americans, Olin Stephens was hard at work developing the lines of *Vim* with ideas gleaned from years of designing and successfully racing the smaller 6-meter class.

Although unsuccessful in America's Cup history, *Vim* was of some significance in the development of the 12-meter class constructed to the International Rule. Built for Harold S. Vanderbilt in 1938, her dimensions were an overall length of 70 feet, a waterline length of 45 feet 3 inches, and a beam of 11 feet 9 inches with a draft of 9 feet 1 inch. The sail area came to 1,817 square feet, and she had a displacement of 60,000 pounds. She was to be the link between regular 12-meter racing of the 1930s and the beginning of a new America's Cup era in the immediate postwar years.

Olin had been helmsman aboard *Ranger* in 1937, but both his and Rod's interest and experience of the smaller-meter yachts stretched back to the early 1920s, when they were still attending high school. They had been introduced to 6-meter sailing by family friend and notable small boat sailor Sherman Hoyt (the bluffing helmsman of Vanderbilt's *Rainbow* in the 1934 J class match against England's T.O.M. Sopwith). Hoyt, who sailed out of the same yacht club at Larchmont, introduced the brothers to 6-meter owner Clinton Crane, who had recently taken delivery of a new six commissioned for a challenge series between the British and Americans. After several amicable sailing matches on Long Island Sound, it was perhaps not too surprising that Rod and Olin's interest in 6-meter racing and design reached almost fanatical proportions. Olin Stephens's first designs were of these small, fast, and handy racing keelboats, and it was only natural that his interest should progress further into the world of 12 meters when the opportunity came along.

Vim was a stripped-out thoroughbred, a tank-tested racing machine with only one purpose in life: to win races. This she did in her first season after being shipped to England for the season in 1939. There she proceeded to thrash the British twelves *Tomahawk*, owned by Sopwith, and *Evaine*.

At the Royal Yacht Squadron in Cowes, it was perfectly clear to keen observers—long before the New York Yacht Club made its successful application to the Supreme Court

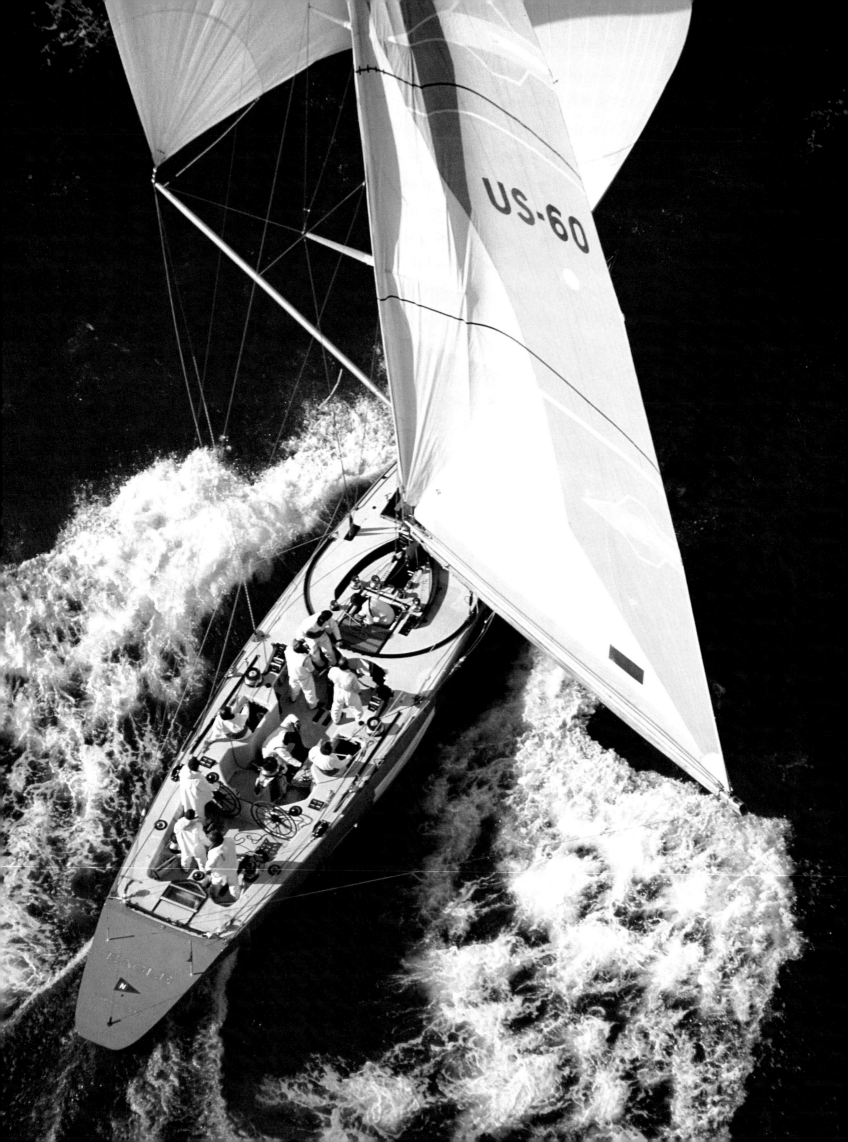

Opposite: Eagle, *designed by Johan Valentijn in 1986. Note the clear deck space and mainsheet trimmers "bunkers."* Right: *Ben Lexcen's successful winged-keel* Australia II, *which, with John Bertrand at the wheel, defeated Dennis Conner's* Liberty *in the 1983 cup match.* Australia II *revolutionized the underwater shape of future 12M yachts.*

of the State of New York for changes in the America's Cup Deed of Gift—that the Americans once again held a decided edge in yacht racing technology.

By comparison with the huge prewar J class, the 12 meters of the fifties were midgets. Surprisingly, quite a fleet of these yachts still raced and came from France, Germany, Italy, and Sweden to meet the Americans and the British on the frequently turbulent Solent waters. At 70 feet overall and with just about an arm's length of freeboard, you could not call a 12-meter magnificent by any stretch of the imagination. They were elegant, yes, and in the right conditions could still provide a spectacle when equally matched.

But in those postwar years, the America's Cup was a dying regatta. The event had long since been staged off Newport, Rhode Island, where there was no towering skyscraper backdrop and where the much-loved (by onlookers) pageantry of support craft and steamers was nonexistent. As a spectator sport, it lacked the glamour of New York Harbor. It had become an event for yachting aficionados only and would stay that way for many years to come.

In 1958, the first challenge since the end of the J class era saw *Vim* and the newly built *Columbia*, also designed by Olin Stephens, racing all summer in an attempt to select a defender against Britain's beautiful, wooden-hulled *Scep-*

tre. Either of the American yachts could have been chosen; there was very little between them, and in the event *Columbia* beat the British yacht 4–0 straight off. That and many of the challenges that followed were runaway successes for the Americans.

The reasons for this were not difficult to pinpoint, even though many cup watchers accurately observed that one or two challengers were actually faster through the water than the Americans. What always saved the day for the Americans was their superiority in sail design, in crew management, and in crew training.

This sorry state of affairs lasted for a very long time, and the only man behind a British effort to realize this before the 1986 effort was the *Victory* syndicate chairman, Peter de Savary. Although *Victory* put up a good showing, serious team managerial problems beset that challenge from its inception.

In the between years, the Australians, the first contenders outside of Britain to challenge for the cup since 1881, made a more determined, somewhat less pedestrian approach in their efforts to take the cup from its pedestal in the NYYC. Their attitude is reflected in a number of ways. They were more aware of the importance of continued crew training, exercising, and general fitness. They learned early (from the

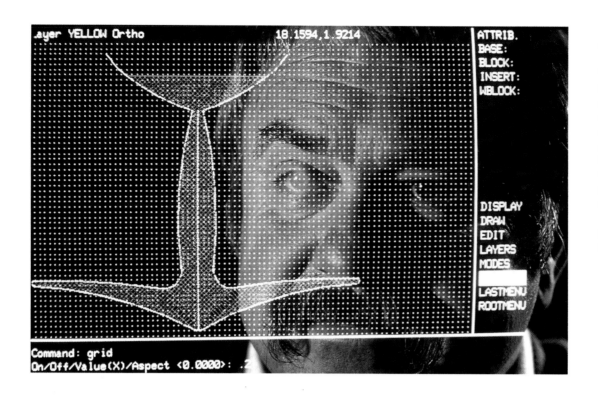

.ayer YELLOW Ortho   18.1594,1.9214

ATTRIB.
BASE:
BLOCK:
INSERT:
WBLOCK:

DISPLAY
DRAW
EDIT
LAYERS
MODES

LASTMENU
ROOTMENU

Command: grid
On/Off/Value(X)/Aspect <0.0000>: .2

Left: *Gary Mull studies the keel design for* Australia II. Below left: *Alan Bond, whose longtime quest to wrest the cup from its New York resting place reached fruition in 1983. He is seen here at the launch of his* Australia IV *in Fremantle in 1986.* Below right: Australia II's *famous winged keel, unveiled at Newport.* Opposite: *Ben Lexcen sails one of his mini 12M replicas of* Australia II *around the harbor of Fremantle in 1986.*

112

Opposite: Australia IV, *whose erratic performance in the defenders' trials made selection of the defender rest with* Kookaburra III. *Right:* Australia III *was the 12M world champion in March 1986; by December of the same year, she was outdated.*

Above, below, and opposite:
*Ben Lexcen was first noticed
as a creative designer while
sailing and drawing the
ubiquitous 18-foot Sydney
skiff. The Ericsson, a very
recent Lexcen design,
competed in the first round
of the Grand Prix sailing event
at Perth.*

Americans) the value of trial horses and match racing against
them. Sydney newspaper proprietor Sir Frank Packer's effort
of 1962 was of the definite opinion that with the best will in
the world, they could not make as big a mess of their
challenge as the British had done in 1958 with *Sceptre*. *Vim*
was chartered for crew training and evaluation, and while
that was going on an unknown Sydney-based naval architect
by the name of Alan Payne was hard at work testing models
at the Stevens Institute tanks in the United States.

Payne went to Sparkman & Stephens, where he found
much help and enthusiasm for the impending Australian
challenge. Indeed, even the New York Yacht Club bent
over backward to help the Sydney Royal Yacht Squadron's
America's Cup committee by agreeing that certain clauses
in the Deed of Gift did not necessarily preclude the use of
some materials and equipment manufactured outside Australia, where, according to the rules, the challenger had to
be designed and built.

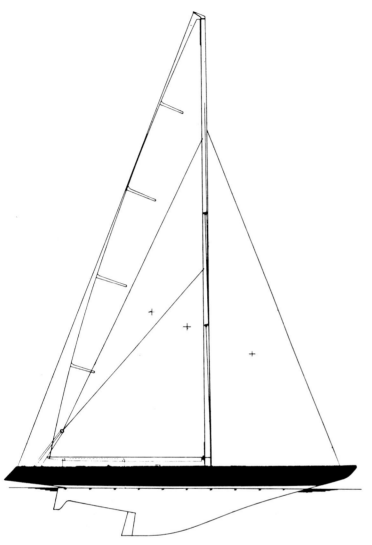

Above: *Sail plan of
Courageous*. Right: *Alan
Payne's* Gretel II *goes through
her paces in Sydney harbor
before being shipped
to America.*

Payne's model-towing experiments in the Hoboken,
New Jersey, tanks were the first real breakthrough in 12-
meter design outside of the United States. The New York
Yacht Club, anxious to inject some excitement back into
the event and give a "sporting" chance to the Aussies,
allowed them to import the best Honduras mahogany as
well as some spar extrusion from the United States. De
Havilland's, the Australian aircraft company, welded and
tapered the masts to aeronautical exactness. If that were not
enough, the NYYC also allowed the Australians to buy
American sailcloth and have their sails made by American
sailmakers at Hood's.

Ted Hood, naval architect, engineer, and sailmaker,
probably influenced the trend of 12M design more than any
other person, except Olin Stephens, from the time the class
was introduced to America's Cup until late in the 1970s. He
designed two of the defense candidates, in 1962 (*Nefertiti*)
and 1977 (*Independence*). He was skipper of *Courageous*

in 1974 with Dennis Conner as starting helmsman. Ted Hood's sailmaking company at Marblehead was at the forefront of 12-meter sail development and also produced and introduced the then-innovative lightweight cloth Dacron, by DuPont, from which all 12-meter sails were cut. Alan Payne investigated every possible angle of 12M design and construction while visiting the United States. The open-handed attitude of the Americans toward the impending Aussie challenge was probably the real breakthrough in terms of future 12-meter development, for without it, that ugly claret jug would probably still be in its old glass case in the New York Yacht Club.

Payne's resulting Gretel was a tank-tested superiority over the American defender Weatherly. She could tack faster, due mainly to her linked set of coffee-grinder winches. She was generally accepted to be faster in a breeze, and in the races against Bus Mosbacher off Newport, Gretel made history in the second race when, after surfing off the top of a wave on a spinnaker run, she went ahead to win. It was the first time since 1934, when Sopwith's Endeavour beat Rainbow, that any challenger had won a race.

Sadly for the Australian effort, Emil Mosbacher's experience and wily tactics saved the day for the defenders. The cup remained in New York. Australia lost because of bad management, not because Gretel was too slow. Payne's boat, given the right weather conditions and a crew with more experience, would have beaten the defender. It was Sir Frank Packer's strange ideas with regard to crew selection that prevented a real team being developed for the challenger. In match racing, the only successful crew is the one that has full confidence in its skipper and the one in which the skipper has the respect of his backer or backers. Challenges from the British in subsequent years failed for precisely the same reasons. This pattern of development can often be seen settling in at the outset, when the campaign begins to gather momentum and the sailing crews are selected for early trials.

The Australians and Sir Frank Packer would have been back for the next round, in 1964, but the British beat him to the challenge. They need not have bothered, however, for with Sovereign, it seemed they had learned nothing from the disaster of Sceptre's humiliating defeat. Another 4–0 win to the Americans in four straight races. From then until the early seventies the America's Cup was plagued with misfit challenges, amateurish dabbles in a field in which the Americans had clear superiority.

The NYYC further revamped the Deed of Gift after Gretel's challenge to effectively block any further cooperation from the Americans. In future, all sails and sail technology, deck furniture, equipment, as well as masts and rigging of

Opposite top: Ted Turner
skippered the converted 12M
American Eagle to a new
Fastnet record in 1971.
Opposite bottom left: Gretel II.
Opposite bottom right:
Australia IV.

American origin were outlawed to any challenger. Further, there was to be no more help from American yacht designers. The foreigners were out on a limb and would have to develop their own technology if they were ever to get a hold on that cup.

Warwick Hood's beautiful pale blue Dame Pattie (named after the prime minister's wife, Dame Pattie Menzies) was the next Australian challenger, in 1967. But she too was given a thrashing and lost four straight races against Intrepid. Undaunted by this fracas, the Sydney newspaper proprietor Sir Frank returned for his second and final attempt with another Payne boat, called Gretel II.

Payne's second challenger had as much potential to win as his first. In the elimination series against Baron Marcel Bich's France, the Europeans were trounced 4–0. But the Australian team management, sails, and their general attitude toward cup racing came a poor second to the Americans, even though the Americans had to go to five races to retain the cup. A virtual avalanche of messages and telegrams from yachting aficionados and sportsmen around the world followed a protest from the Australians at the way in which the rerun of the abandoned second race was handled that year. World opinion was such that it forced the New York Yacht Club to reconsider the formula for handling protests, and ultimately the club relinquished control of the committee and agreed to the establishment of an international jury.

In Western Australia, the city of Perth's only claim to fame had occurred some years before: a minor involvement in the world's first manned spaceflight. The city lights were turned on so that astronaut John Glenn might see them from space. Civilized Australia was several thousand miles to the east. Sydney was Australia, and to much of the rest of the world, Australia was Sydney. In the outback of Western Australia, Perth was nothing more than a collection of architectural Victoriana surrounded by fields of clapboard houses with corrugated tin roofs.

Alan Bond, whose name would eventually dominate newspaper headlines and the pages of yachting journals worldwide, emigrated to Australia from Ealing in London. He set up shop as a sign writer, and it is claimed that one of his masterpieces features an Australian dingo painted on the side of a flour mill overlooking the Indian Ocean near Fremantle.

Bond, a brash and somewhat abrasive person typifying European comic-book cameos of the "outback Aussie," soon tired of painting other people's names and moved into the world of real estate. History has it that Alan Bond was called to the bedside of an ailing Sir Frank Packer and was told not to give up with the cup until he had won it for Australia.

Bond purchased Gretel II as a trial horse and hired another unknown by the name of Bob Miller to design his second boat, Southern Cross. Miller is a New South Wales–born Australian, now in his fifties. He changed his name to Ben Lexcen after falling out with a business partner in the

Seen here at Cowes in 1977, Lexcen's famous maxi-racer Ballyhoo *heralded a new concept in ocean racing design.*

middle seventies. He began his yachting career as a sail-maker and progressed to crewing on as many different classes as time would allow. He represented Australia at several Olympic Games and, after a period designing those overcanvased 18-foot Sydney skiffs and dinghies, he drew two yachts for the Admiral's Cup series of 1973, *Ginkgo* and *Apollo II*. Both of them performed with spectacular success, and had the Aussies won the Admiral's Cup that year, these designs might have brought Lexcen more work.

He designed six Sydney-Hobart Race winners and revolutionized the maxi class in 1974 with a yacht named *Ballyhoo*. He is best known for his association with Bond's 12 meters, and in addition to *Southern Cross* and the America's Cup winner *Australia II*, he also designed *Australia, Challenge 12, South Australia;* and the very recent 12-meter world champion *Australia III*. *Australia IV* was Lexcen's latest creation for the Alan Bond defense syndicate. Sadly, Lexcen's innovative and creative ability was overshadowed by a younger personage in the shape of Iain Murray.

Ben Lexcen's approach to designing 12-meter yachts was always innovative. If Olin Stephens designed more American defenders by sticking to convention, Lexcen must have brought more creativity to the art of drawing these cumbersome race boats. His first 12 meter for Alan Bond, nicknamed "the stone banana" because of its bright yellow hull and near disastrous sinking after a 4–0 defeat by *Coura-*

geous, was long and completely flush-decked. In addition, *Southern Cross* sported a peculiar, blunted nose, called a knuckle-back, that shortened the displacement controlling measurement waterline length but still retained the yacht's sailing length above the waterline. Bond called this his secret weapon, but it served no good purpose. *Southern Cross* was simply not fast enough to beat Olin Stephens's conventional twelve, and it was apparent that more work needed to be carried out testing models.

After the 1974 race was over, Lexcen himself freely admitted that he had put too much faith in the results of tank testing, but he was still convinced that his chopped-off bow was an important feature—so much so that he continued with it in successors to the stone banana. When Alan Bond decided to challenge for the cup again in 1977, Lexcen was commissioned to design a new twelve. His assistant was a young Dutch-born designer whose most recent previous experience had included a stint working at the Sparkman & Stephens design office.

Lexcen and Johan Valentijn worked together testing models at the Delft tank in Holland. Lexcen's new *Australia* was computed to be six seconds a mile faster than the American *Courageous*, but Ted Turner, who skippered the American yacht with a near-perfect suit of sails and had spent months training his crew to near perfection, still managed to hold off the Aussie attack, and in spite of some very close racing, at no mark did *Australia* manage to get ahead of her rival in

Right: Lionheart. Following pages: Sverige *(left), designed by Sweden's Pelle Petterson, racing with* Constellation, *the 1964 Stephens-designed defender, off Brighton, England, in 1979.*

the finals. Bond returned home again; lesser men would have crawled into a hole to hide.

Alan Bond may have received another knockdown, but he certainly wasn't beaten or out of the running. His real-estate business had benefited not a little from his involvement in the cup, and in 1980 he again channeled his efforts for another crack at the event. Ben Lexcen, always confident that the hand-me-down rig from *Southern Cross* had been *Australia's* undoing in 1977, was asked by Bond to make modifications to the boat rather than design a new one.

In England, Tony Boyden was mounting a challenge with a Howlett-designed twelve called *Lionheart.* This effort was to be beset with managerial problems, but for all that, *Lionheart* had potential. In her many trial outings in the Solent during the early summer of 1980, the first British twelve for many years sported an unusual, bendy mast, a rule-cheater that allowed several hundred extra square feet of canvas to be hoisted, giving the yacht better speed than her opponents in light airs.

The American defenders were skeptical of this asset, probably because there was too little time for them to develop their own bendy rig. But Lexcen was quick to see the potential advantages and soon had a similar rig hoisted on the modified *Australia.* A 4-meter-long fiberglass tip was added to a conventional mast, giving not only the extra sail area necessary for extra speed in light weather but also a more efficient masthead from an aeronautical standpoint.

In the elimination rounds, the Lexcen boat knocked out Baron Bich's *France III* and then almost as easily disposed of the British. The final match, between Dennis Conner's *Freedom* and *Australia,* produced a series of races unequaled for excitement in the previous contemporary history of the cup. It was at last clearly apparent that someone other than America had an edge; 1980 was the year the myth that American 12-meter crews were unbeatable finally went out the window. Bond and Lexcen came away beaten 4–1, but now they had had the taste of victory. Had time not run out on another race, they would have won that too by a staggering 700-meter lead.

Bond wasted no time in making his challenge for the 1983 event, announcing at the final press conference in the Newport Armory in 1980 that he would be back in 1983 with Ben Lexcen, and with *Australia's* sail-trimmer, John Bertrand, as skipper of a new boat.

Bertrand and Lexcen had worked together previously on masts for *Southern Cross.* Now they were to become part of a formidable team in which every Bond-picked member contributed in no small way to the eventual undoing of American domination. Lexcen was given virtual carte blanche to go away and try out anything that took his fancy that he believed might make for a faster, more maneuverable yacht.

CHAPTER 8

For the Cup

Ben Lexcen is the archetypal dreamer, the "artist" yacht designer who has never been afraid of his own creativity but always confident that what he had dreamed up would work. The *Apollos, Ginkgo,* and his maxi yacht *Ballyhoo* of 1974 are testimony to an original and unique flair for designing world beaters.

When *Ballyhoo* was launched in 1974, she was the largest and most expensive maxi yacht in Australia. Built for Jack Rooklyn at a cost of $AUS300,000, *Ballyhoo* was 72 feet overall with a beam of 15 feet and a draft of 9 feet 9 inches. For two years after her launching, she was at the forefront of maxi racing, narrowly missing victory to *Ondine* in her first Sydney-Hobart but beating *Kialoa* and *Windward Passage* on other racing circuits of the world and eventually taking line honors in the 1976 Sydney-Hobart.

In 1980, the British devised an ingenious, bendy top for the mast of their America's Cup challenger, *Lionheart,* which allowed a useful extra area of mainsail to be set, thus giving the boat more speed. Lexcen was not slow in copying the idea, and he and two others of the Australian forty-man syndicate worked frantically to prepare a bendy topmast for *Australia.* Their one win in light airs was enough to prove the point.

In 1981, Lexcen flew to Holland, where he spent several months working on ingenious ideas using the facilities of the Netherlands Ship Model Basin. An old friend, Peter Van Oossanen, had encouraged Lexcen that the only way to

Left: *Dennis Conner and the crew of* Stars & Stripes *receive a rapturous welcome in Fremantle's harbor following their victory.* Above: Italia.

find out if some of his weird and quite strange ideas for 12-meter keels would work was by testing them scientifically. The New York Yacht Club granted the Bond syndicate special permission to use the tank-testing facilities at Wageningen, where Van Oossanen worked as one of Holland's top ship-design researchers.

For Lexcen, being able to use these sophisticated facilities was akin to finding a pot of gold at the end of a rainbow. Sydney's tank-testing facilities were basic by comparison, and the largest models were only 8 feet long. In Holland, Ben Lexcen roughed out drawings, and expert draftsmen turned them into plans for 24-foot models. By towing and inclining the models from the mast, a great deal of data was scientifically fed into computers, and from this, Lexcen was able to compare more exactly how each of his ideas had performed.

In the beginning, he drew a conventional-looking twelve

and tested it with a variety of keels. *Challenge 12* was the result. She was Alan Bond's safe bet for the 1983 challenge, a conventional hull with a fat keel. Later she was sold to the Royal Yacht Club of Victoria, the members of which took it to Newport and failed.

With time to spare in Holland and the facilities of the tank-testing basin still at his disposal, Lexcen was able to test several of his winged-keel theories. Initially, the keel was simply an upside-down version of the conventional type sans wings, a design configuration he attributes to the keel of the Flying Fifteen designed by Uffa Fox. At first, the tank results were not very spectacular, apart from the fact that the model went adrift while being towed and virtually demolished half the Netherlands Ship Model Basin's stock of ship models.

After hasty repairs had been made, the new model was put through its paces with spectacular results. The wings were added later after studying the performance of the Lear Jet executive airplane. Once a position, overall size, and angle of dihedral had been established through a trial-and-error process, *Australia II* was on the drawing board. To Lexcen's amazement, Alan Bond rapidly warmed to the idea of a winged keel. Though supposedly a "secret" weapon, quite a large number of people in Europe knew of the wings. Peter de Savary, who had underwritten the cost of the *Victory '83* challenge was not slow in trying them out on his own yacht. His mistake was simply that *Victory '83's* wings were not large enough.

The British lost in the elimination races. *Australia II* went on to defeat the Americans for the first time in 132 years, a winning streak so long that many observers had come to believe that the spell could never be broken. Skipper John Bertrand had to fight hard, and Dennis Conner, the first man to lose the cup, fought even harder. For the first time ever, the match series went to a race-off in race seven.

In many respects, it is a wonder that the cup remained bolted to the floor of the New York Yacht Club for as long as it did. Doyen of 12-meter design Olin Stephens had long been a keen supporter of tank testing, ever since the days of *Ranger* and its designer Starling Burgess. But conservatism paralyzed the Americans. Olin Stephens produced many fine cup yachts, and six times they were successful defenders: *Columbia* (1958), *Constellation* (1964), *Intrepid* (1967), *Courageous* (1974 and 1977), and *Freedom* (1980).

Intrepid was an Olin Stephens masterpiece. He used an idea originally conceived by Nathaniel Herreshoff to split the keel away from the rudder, thus creating the fin-keeled twelve. She had a snubbed-off bow and huge volume in the hull in front of the rudder. Minneford's at City Island built the hull. All the winches were placed below deck level. *Intrepid* became a benchmark in 12-meter design. She won in 1967 and again in 1970.

Ben Lexcen's *Australia II* became the new benchmark of 1983. In 1986, every one of the seventeen challengers and defenders sported a variation of the Lexcen winged keel. Many of these variations were subtle; some were simple, safe, copies. Ian Howlett's British *White Crusader* was a classic example of the conservative challenger, aesthetically more pleasing to the eye than many of her competitors but obsolete before she was off the drawing board. Her stablemate, "The Hippo," designed by model yacht designer David Hollom in conjunction with Stephen Wallis and Herbert Pearcy, was a radical departure from that same safe conservatism that only three years previously had caused outrage behind closed doors of the New York Yacht Club.

"The Hippo" never got to the starting line, either because of British conservatism or because not too many people had discovered how to make the yacht go consistently well enough. She stayed at home, her long, chiseled stern jutting from the pen in defiance, while Harold Cudmore went out and did his damnedest to get the safe bet surfing. He too failed by a thread.

Johan Valentijn's *Eagle*, probably the most exciting-looking twelve with her larger than life eagle graphics painted

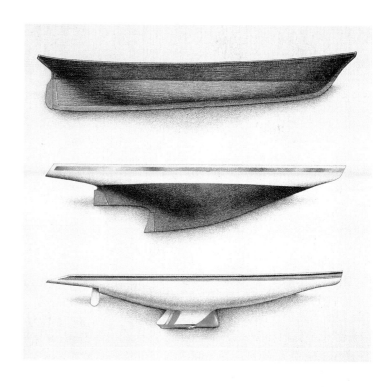

Opposite: *Stars & Stripes's hull under construction at Derecktor's yard. Special framing techniques were used to give the hull extra stiffness.* Above: *The development of hull design from the 1851 schooner* America *(top) to* Intrepid, *by Olin Stephens, to the New York Yacht Club's* America II.

along her topsides, soon acquired the nickname of "Beagle." Toward the end, her beautiful keel was butchered, and she reappeared with a look-alike surfboard attached to the bottom. If anything, she became more sluggish. Asked by a reporter what he would do with the yacht when it failed to make the semifinals of the challengers' elimination races, skipper Rod Davis is said to have declared that he would cut it up with a chain saw and dump the pieces in Johan Valentijn's backyard.

America II, pride of the New York Yacht Club, was another challenger that went out in the third round. Skipper John Kolius, a tall and amiable Texan who had spent three years campaigning from Fremantle, was not around long enough to make any comment on what would happen to his yacht. The New York Yacht Club had—unwisely, in this case—chosen Sparkman & Stephens as the designer. *America II* was just another copy of *Australia II*, the top yacht in

Left: *When the Stars & Stripes victory celebrations were over, a portion of the boat's Roman-nose keel was unveiled; not exposed, however, were the revolutionary, swept-back wings on the keel's aft end.* Opposite: *Britain's 12M challenger* White Crusader, *designed by Ian Howlett.* Following pages: *KZ-7, or "Kiwi Magic," was one of three glass-fiber boats designed by Ron Holland, Bruce Farr, Laurie Davidson, and Russell Bowler for the New Zealand challenge.*

the 12M Worlds Cup held off Fremantle in March 1986, but by the antipodean summer of the same year already retired to a museum in Canberra, outclassed and outdated.

At the end, the three *America*s sat forlornly on the hard standing of Fremantle's Challenger Harbor, a monument to old technology. *Heart of America*, campaigned vigorously by the Chicago Yacht Club skipper Buddy Melges, had given a good fight, but despite her growing wings—they had expanded with the addition of winglets on the wings and then tiplets on the winglets—she was out too. *French Kiss*, magnificently steered by downhill-racer Marc Pajot, ended her campaign with a chopped-off stern, a last-ditch attempt by designer Philippe Briand perhaps to save weight. She surfed well in the sometimes heavy seas and high winds off Fremantle but was still no match for the plastic fantastic *Kiwi Magic* from New Zealand.

The Kiwi boat had seemed unbeatable at one stage. She had won all but one race of the three elimination rounds, resulting in a total score of 33–1. She lost once to *Stars & Stripes*, the banana-shaped, gunsmoke-blue threat from San Diego steered by the man who had lost the cup, Dennis Conner.

In heavy weather, *KZ-7*'s skipper, Chris Dickson, so confident of both his and the boat's ability to win, was accused more than once of sandbagging in some of the races; that is, holding back on the tail of his opponent and then coming for the kill at the last moment. At press conferences, Dickson avoided direct confrontation with that question or flatly denied the suggestion.

And, as in Newport, so in Fremantle. The "Keelgate" controversy, which surrounded *Australia II*'s pedigree and left a sour taste for everyone to savor, became, in Fremantle, the "Glassgate" affair. New Zealand had the only glass-fiber-constructed twelve. Dissatisfied with the way she had been built, Conner's syndicate called for core samples of the hull. When the request was refused, Conner denied he had called the New Zealand syndicate cheats.

The sourness got worse. The Royal New Zealand Yacht Squadron wrote defiantly to the San Diego Yacht Club refusing entry to members of the latter who might turn up for a beer. In New Zealand, hype went ridiculous. Even before Dickson had won his match against *French Kiss* in the semifinals, reports were filtering back to Fremantle that real estate in the Auckland area had doubled in price virtually overnight. A young Dunedin couple, smitten by Chris Dickson's ability, named their newborn daughter after the yacht—Corazon Takau Rose Julliet James KZ7 Cavanagh.

KZ-7, as the yacht was officially named, was the result of a two-and-a-half-year development program that saw the arrival of *KZ-3* and *KZ-5* long before the famous *7*. Three of New Zealand's top designers, Ron Holland, Laurie Davidson, and Bruce Farr, all of them acknowledged as the top designers in the field of contemporary International Offshore Rule (IOR) design for over a decade, were hired by the New Zealand challenge syndicate.

Bruce Farr, who first came to fame in 1976 during the One-Ton Cup world championship off Marseilles with a radical upstart called *45 deg South*, had already expanded

lost to experience. He made some goofy mistakes, like running into a buoy on the last leg of a race while hot on Conner's tail.

To any lay observer, it might have seemed that Conner simply had the better boat. He did. But he also had the better crew and the better mind. It had often been said that Dickson's opponent was the best 12-meter skipper in the world. Who could doubt that now? And yet, the New Zealander has a quality unmatched even by Conner. He has what is known as the killer instinct. In dispatches to the U.S. West Coast, one writer likened the appearance of the 25-year-old Dickson to that of a U-boat commander. He seemed too young to be trading tacks with America's Cup veterans like Dennis Conner and Tom Blackaller. Dickson was unconcerned. He calculated everything to kill off the opponent, including the will of the opposing skipper to fight. Dickson's apparent sandbagging techniques looked as if they were designed simply as a psychological tactic. Aside from any sailing tactic designed to pinch the wind of the yacht ahead, Dickson reveled in the "I'm-coming-to-get-you!" psyche out. He sailed KZ-7 so close to the stern of his opponents that on some occasions the effect was unnerving on spectators. Imagine how it affected the crew on the yacht pursued. Dickson invariably came through an opening at the last moment to prove yet again that he was a force to be reckoned with.

Conner was never slow to acknowledge the threat of the Kiwis. Like many experienced and less exuberant Americans, however, Conner exuded a kind of awesome confidence in his own ability and in that of his crew and boats to do the job he had come to do—take the cup home. Since his involvement with Courageous in 1974, Conner had accumulated 8,000 hours of sea time in 12-meter yachts. Tactician to Conner, Tom Whidden, said, "He's the best in the world at what he does." Whidden would know. He sailed with Conner in 1980 on Freedom, on Liberty in 1983, and was back again with Stars & Stripes off Fremantle.

What must not be overlooked either is Conner's obsession with winning the cup back for America. He was already noted in the history books as the man who lost it—three and a half years after that sad and dismal affair on Rhode Island Sound, the smiling Californian tucked the "auld mug" under his arm and walked up the steps of a Continental Airlines charter flight at Perth airport, bound for Washington, a meeting with the president, and another mention in the history books as the man who won back the world's oldest sporting trophy.

For the first time since 1851, America was in a position where it had to challenge for the cup instead of defending it. Conner brought together a team of the very best of management, crew, sailmaking, and design that America could muster and put it all together under the auspices of the Sail America Foundation. Its president, Malin Burnham, is chairman of First National Bank and a number of other corporate organizations. He was a Star Class world champion, the skipper of Enterprise in 1977, and Dennis Conner's practice

skipper aboard Freedom in 1980 and Liberty in 1983.

John Marhsall, the design coordinator, a former mainsail trimmer on both Conner's 1980 and 1983 defenders, a former president of North Sails, a sailmaker, sailor, and scientist, pulled together a remarkable design team for the three Stars & Stripes yachts built by Robert E. Derecktor. Britton Chance, Jr., with over 25 years experience in the field of 12M design, was previously involved with Chanceggar, Mariner, and Intrepid, the Sparkman & Stephens breakthrough he redesigned for the 1970 defense. He has also had notable successes in the field of 5.5.-meter designs.

Bruce Nelson, a 34-year-old from the challenging syndicate's hometown base of San Diego, has been designing yachts since 1977. An experienced sailor, he designed the IOR yachts High Roler, Stars & Stripes, and Sleeper, all Admiral's Cup yachts in 1985. His Swiftsure was the Transpac winner of the same year, and in the following year he produced Crazy Horse, overall winner of the Kenwood Cup.

The third member of the Sail America Foundation's design team was David Pedrick, who since 1972 had accumulated a mass of 12M design knowledge. While chief designer at Sparkman & Stevens he headed the design team for Courageous (1974) and Enterprise (1977). That year he founded his own design firm and drew the lines for Clipper (1980) and Defender (1983). A graduate of the Webb Institute of Naval Architecture, Pedrick's IOR successes include the beautiful Nirvana and Sovereign.

This formidable design team, collectively endowed with more 12M-design experience than any of the other challenging syndicates, had but one aim: to produce the world's fastest 12-meter yacht. They applied American space technology and by using advanced computer simulations were able to test more than 100 hull and keel configurations before selecting the three they figured would be most likely to fulfill their aims. In one year, the team effectively tested more designs than had been tested throughout the entire 134-year history of the America's Cup.

So confident were they at the end that Derecktor's New York boatyard at Mamaroneck was commissioned to build the three 12 meters named Stars & Stripes 1, 2, and 3. Derecktor had earlier revamped the hull of a 1983 defense contender, Spirit of America, which was used to test some of the computer ideas. Spirit of America trialed against the 1983 loser, Liberty, at that time the second-fastest 12 meter in the world (Australia II was faster). Spirit of America outpaced the loser. Stars & Stripes I outpaced Spirit of America, and so it went.

Robert E. Derecktor founded his boatyard in 1947 and has been acclaimed as one of the finest aluminium yacht builders in the world. The same yard also built USA for Tom Blackaller and the St. Francis Yacht Club challenge. Stars & Stripes was built in a little under three months. Derecktor used an innovative longitudinal framing system with increased vertical frames instead of employing the more traditional transverse framing method. This construction

Opposite: Stars & Stripes *in action in the Indian Ocean off Fremantle. Above: The yacht Club Costa Smeralda (Challenger of Record for the 1987 America's Cup) entry* Azzurra *was designed by Stuido's Valicelli and Sciomachen.* Azzurra *was one of the slowest 12Ms afloat off Fremantle. Here her crew celebrate after winning a match against* Challenge France. *Right:* Kookaburra II.

technique resulted in an altogether stiffer boat with less plate buckling and other distortions caused by the heavy seas off Fremantle.

While nearly all of the remaining yachts gathered at Fremantle for the 1986 eliminations and defense trials sported some sort of variation of Lexcen's winged keel, *Stars & Stripes*, when finally unveiled for the world to see, confirmed abounding rumors of a Roman-nose configuration. John Marhsall's design team had successfully found a way of blending the old with the new in producing a keel that looked suspiciously like a slimmed down version of the common, or garden, bulbous bow sported by supertankers and other commercial vessels. The Roman-nose shape was, in fact, nothing new.

If a bulbous bow is viewed in profile, the Roman-nose shape can be clearly seen from the cutwater downward. Chance, Pedrick, and Nelson simply did the obvious thing. They explored the possibilities of a squeezed version of a bulbous bow, adapting it to fit the configuration of the now common Lexcen keel while all the time testing a variety of trailing edges to produce the best effective speed increase. The maneuverability of *Stars & Stripes* came from a finely balanced rudder placed well aft and quite large winglets that protruded in swept-back fashion from the trailing edge of the keel.

The yacht's bananalike sheerline was completely effective in keeping *Stars & Stripes* dry in the 6- to 7-foot seas experienced in the Indian Ocean. Her keel also seemed to act as the fore and aft pivot point of the hull, sucking the hull into a hole as it was pushed forward by the best suit of sails ever made for a twelve. In fact, it was Tom Whidden who maintained near the end of the series in 1986 that the yacht's extra speed had come from her sails, not the etched go-faster 3M plastic sheeting that had been stuck to her hull.

When *Stars & Stripes* moved forward at speed in heavy weather, the hull appeared to be the driving force. You didn't look at the sails. You looked at the way the hull leaped forward, snuck close to the deck like a greyhound in full flight. Other boats hobbyhorsed in the choppy conditions, took water over the decks by the bucketful, and often seemed slower on the windward legs; Conner aimed higher

Above: USA *(left) and*
Stars & Stripes *were both*
built by Robert Derecktor.

Opposite: *On-board view*
of deck arrangements on
Stars & Stripes.

and moved faster.

Dennis Conner was eventually successful. On the one occasion when the Australian defender *Kookaburra III* pulled off a head start and looked set to take the first leg, sheer speed took *Stars & Stripes* into the commanding position. The final match races were hardly ever close, except for the starts, and even then, challenger and defender took opposite sides of the course for the most part. The defender's position was tenuous: her skipper, Iain Murray, is one of the most agreeable yachtsmen, the best kind of loser, and he remained objective throughout the series, sailed the best he could, but candidly acknowledged that Conner had the faster boat.

After all the money has been spent, the sum total of the America's Cup's worth remains simply a boat race. Technology may have advanced a little. New benchmarks are created, and the whole circus begins again. In 1935, C.P. Burgess, brother of the then best known designer of J class yachts, said of them that they "bore not the slightest resemblance to any useful craft in the world. But having damned them, I must confess to an absorbing interest in the problems set by these extraordinary vessels. They have the fascination of sin." Those sentiments can be aptly applied to the 12-meter yacht, a vessel so specialized that it is virtually useless for all but the extraordinary jousts of the America's Cup.

It has often been said that there is nothing new under the sun. However, 12-meter-yacht design is something else. The reason such yachts are racing at all today has to do with colossal sums of money contributed by sponsors to beget lineage, mentions, and visual public contact through television.

The America's Cup regatta is a one-of-a-kind rally. There is no comparable sporting event, no comparable yachting event, no event that stirs the blood and emotions of syndicate bosses, skippers, crews, and spectators to such heights. The America's Cup regatta of the 1980s and the 1990s is almost certainly the costliest sporting event ever staged. In 1986–87, syndicate budgets reached a staggering $25 million Australian dollars. Before that event was barely won by a no-holds-barred *Stars & Stripes* team, the losing Australian defense syndicate boss announced an unbelievable $50 million budget for his next challenge.

The lay reader may well ask what all this is about. Why do such huge sums of money need to be spent in the first place, when, as the 1986 challengers from New Zealand showed the world, plastic boats can provide the necessary high level of competition? The reason is simple and has to do only with corporate hucksterism, the on-board race cam, and television viewers. For the first time in its history, the 12-meter battles fought on the ocean were brought into the living rooms of millions of viewers who had probably never seen a yacht race before, let alone the world's premier yachting event. Large audiences command high prices for advertising space. Sponsors, sure of millions of dollars' worth of prime-time viewing for a tenth of its normal cost, will be only too happy to support challenging syndicates whose only real objective is winning the cup.

Opposite: *The Philippe Briand-designed* French Kiss *being chased by* America II *during the elimination series off Fremantle.* Right: *Dennis Conner, the man who lost and won the cup. His grim determination to win back the cup in 1987 paid off after a long and arduous three-year training program.* Following pages: Stars & Stripes.

CHAPTER 9

The Sun Is Shining, the Sky Is Blue

Leaning on the weathered gunwale of a wreck near Salinas on the island of Lanzarote, clear, warm water lapping at my ankles, I experienced yet again the burning desire to be afloat, gently guiding my newfound Iberian prodigy through the deep Atlantic swells to other islands, tropical coastlines, and unexplored shores far over the horizon. This desire was not born out of a love for the sea, particularly, but more out of a love for the beautiful things that are sometimes to be found floating on it.

Few modern sailboats have the elegant curving lines of many of their workboat ancestors. There on the beach at Salinas lay a prime example of the kind of craft whose design had remained basically the same for hundreds of years. The gentle sweep of the sheerline up toward a flared prow that added buoyancy to a plunging forefoot; sea kindly and dry on deck in the long swells of the Atlantic and plenty of unobstructed room for her crew to work in. How she differed from her sisters of northern Europe, with their slab sides and narrow forward sections designed to slice through the short, choppy seas of the Continental shelf.

Left: *The Round the Island Race draws over 1,000 competitors of all types to race over a 60-mile course.* Above: Newcastle Brown, *a wooden-hulled Folkboat, at the start of the 1985 Round Britain Race.*

Opposite: Madcap, a converted Bristol Channel pilot cutter. Long-distance cruising enthusiasts appreciate such traditional working craft for their seaworthiness and large, below-decks accommodation. Above: Astrid, an Etchells 22, is a high-tech racing machine. Right: Viking, a custom-built Greek cruising yacht developed on the lines of a traditional caique hull.

The further afield one looks, the more stimulating and generally pleasing are working hulls. National traits are easy to spot, something that cannot honestly be said of pleasure boats, the designs of which seem to be fairly rigidly fixed around the primary requisite of more accommodation space. That the finished product is called a yacht is in my view an affront to the capabilities of contemporary designers; very few actually bear much resemblance to the kind of proper yacht tradition tells us is desirable.

Expanding populations, increased wealth, more leisure time, all are contributory factors to the increased popularity of boating. The production cruising yacht is as much an accountant's nightmare as it is a designer's attempt to reconcile his own artistic bent with the demands of the manufacturer. In many cases, performance takes a poor second place to accommodation requirements. Adequate performance means that the boat will sail moderately on most points of wind, but anyone expecting more than that is looking in the wrong place.

A great many production cruisers are not produced for the discerning sailor, but for a market whose idea of sailing is a weekend sat on the end of a marina pier. The apparent ineptitude of some designers and builders, who year after year seem helplessly bound to promote the idea that boats are for sitting in, not sailing in, is exasperating, to say the least. It is a great pity that there is not more recognition of the fact that boats can be designed to please the eye as well as the pocket, and that they can be built to provide comfortable floating homes as well as to give the kind of practical performance that might encourage people to use them.

This is one area of yacht design and construction that is not intimately entwined with racing success. The majority of small family cruising yachts are easily likened more to a floating caravan, and until the demand in that sector of yachting veers more toward performance at sea and away from the requisites of accommodation, it is likely to remain pretty much as it is, stagnating in certain quarters, becoming more outrageous in others.

Consequently, in reading further, some readers may feel deprived, and possibly even dismayed to find that, with very few exceptions, much of the remainder of this work deals with yacht designers who have marked the pages of contemporary yachting history with original and outstanding racing yachts.

The cruising spin-offs from some of these designs are already legendary, and where possible some have been included to lend contrast. For the most part, however, it is each year's new batch of racing machines that has maintained that horizon of jagged peaks.

To gain some perspective, I turn back the clock to October 27, 1972. On this day, yachting lost its most remarkable and colorful genius. Uffa Fox left this world for another at the age of 74. His legacy was huge, a myriad of influential designs and so many successes in racing that one does not know where or how to count them all. Uffa Fox, sailor, architect, author, lecturer, and broadcaster, a celebrity full of fun and good humor, rubbed shoulders with royalty but was simply "Uffa" to everyone who knew him. These few paragraphs can only scratch the surface of that legend. Whole books have been devoted to Uffa's contribution to our world, but the reader is still left gasping for more.

His life was inextricably entwined with Cowes, the Isle of Wight, and sailing. A prolific and imaginative designer, Uffa Fox was responsible for some of the fastest dinghies and keelboats afloat. Thousands of sailing dinghies around the world were designed to plans following Uffa's introduction of the 4.3-meter *Avenger,* a boat with which he won 52 races out of 57 in 1928. Later, he applied his techniques to the design of what must now be considered one of the most elegant keelboats afloat, the Flying Fifteen. *Coweslip,* the most famous of these yachts, was owned and helmed by His Royal Highness Prince Philip, who hardly ever sailed in it without Uffa as his crew. They had many notable successes, and it may well have been that pedigree that caused Ben Lexcen to take a closer look at the Flying Fifteen keel. This design has a 6-meter planing hull ballasted with a 400-pound bulb attached to a fin keel. At one point, more than 2,000 Flying Fifteens were registered with the class association, sailing at over 50 centers in Britain and 30 more in other countries.

Keelboat is a term often loosely used to describe any craft with a fixed, ballasted keel, rather than the lifting daggerboard or centerboard more commonly found in smaller one- and two-man dinghies. Keelboats can measure anything from 15 feet to 70 feet, an example of the latter being the New York Yacht Club One-Design, designed by Nat Herreshoff and built in 1900. Provided the yacht has no coach roof protecting the crew from the elements and

Modern glass-fiber production cruising yachts are designed to meet strict market needs; emphasis is on accommodation, usually the main selling point.

Left: *X class one-designs have a great following on both sides of the Atlantic. Originally designed and built in 1909, they are popular family-owned keelboat racers. Below: The Flying Fifteen Sediki in a flurry of spume and spray off Cowes. Right: Victory class yachts, a later design than the X class keelboat, are seen here sailing off Gibraltar.*

provided it can meet any of the aforementioned conditions, "keelboat" is the category into which it fits.

In the early days of yachting, the traditional OD keelboat of between 20 and 35 feet was perhaps the most popular. The X one-designs are the oldest keelboat class still sailing in England and in a way typify the kind of lines that were fashionable just after the turn of the century. Drawn by Alfred Westmacott, a resident of the Isle of Wight, the X was first built in 1909 and continues to race in large numbers nigh on 80 years later. In 1977, 73 of these craft competed in the annual Cowes Week Regatta.

Westmacott was responsible for a number of other successful Solent designs of which some, like the Sunbeams, are still occasionally built today. The Camper & Nicholson Redwings and the Portsmouth Victory class, which can also be found sailing in the Mediterranean, make up the fleets of nonhandicap classes that add colorful dimension to a modern international regatta.

These older designs are not used only for racing. Many of the 20-foot XODs are family owned and sailed. They are ideal day boats, and not one of them is known to have

capsized or foundered. Some have even made spectacular ocean passages. *X67* was sailed single-handed from Falmouth to Bordeaux and then back to Hamble. In the United States, some 450 X class boats exist, though these are slightly smaller, at 16 feet, and are called Inland Yachting Association Scows. They were first built and designed in 1934.

OLYMPICS

Sailing first appeared as part of the Olympic Games at Meulan on the Seine near Paris in 1900, but it began to feature regularly only from 1908. The games that year were held in London, and the sailing was held at Cowes. It was at this time that the first international rating rule came into effect with 12M, 8M, 7M, and 6M classes. The meter and square meter classes prevailed variously until 1948, when Swallows and Dragons were adopted as Olympic racing classes in the heavy fixed-keel division. By 1962, most of the smaller meter classes had fallen by the wayside, and the International Yacht Racing Union, which was formed in 1907 after a meeting by yachting representatives from eleven countries and which is one of three international bodies that now supervises yacht racing around the world, began to look for a suitable class of keelboat to replace the aging 5.5-meter class.

In Norway, the experienced and knowledgeable Jan Hermann Linge had already begun working on a replacement for the class. His design was slightly smaller and had been conceived for glass-fiber production. A wooden prototype was first built, and following successful trials, five of these new three-man keelboats were sailed and evaluated by the IYRU through the 1966 season. By now, production of the new boats was well under way, and after further IYRU trials in 1967, the Soling was given international class status.

By the following year, over 300 of these fast, new boats were sailing all over the world. Such was their popularity that the International Olympic Committee selected the Soling to replace the 5.5 meter for the Olympiad in 1972. Among the twenty-seven entries that year was four-time Olympic gold medalist Paul Elvstrom. He was beaten by Harry Melges, Jr., Stig Wennerstroem, and David Miller of the United States, Sweden, and Canada respectively. Since Jan Linge launched the first yacht, some 2,500 Solings have been registered as being sailed in over forty countries, with the largest concentrations in Canada and Germany.

Opposite top: Soling, *designed by Jan Linge, in action during a Weymouth Olympic week meeting.* Opposite bottom: *45 deg. South, a Bruce Farr-designed one-tonner at Marseilles in 1976.* Below: *Loading stores for a weekend cruise down the Florida Keys in a bilge-keeled Jaguar 27 production crusier.*

OFFSHORE ONE-DESIGN

During the mid 1970s, the regatta fleets at Cowes grew to enormous proportions and caused confusion, antagonism, and exasperation to the organizers of the Admiral's Cup, which was sailed in the same waters off Cowes biennially. Yacht clubs and race committees were quick to encourage the idea of one-design offshore racing yachts, partially in the hope that major international regattas like the Admiral's Cup could be run in truly spectacular style away from the main area of regatta yachting and at some other time in the season.

Within a few years, offshore one-design (OOD) racing in Europe had gathered momentum. From the outset, there was very little hope of an event like the Admiral's Cup ever being sailed in OODs, but the various early suggestions that it should brought spin-offs in other directions. Small groups of one-design owners organized events that helped to promote their ideas.

The American Congressional Cup contest, held annually off Long Beach, California, was imitated in Britain but on a much smaller scale. The idea was also received enthusiastically in France, where sailing had become a national sport in the wake of Frenchman Eric Tabarly's many shorthanded successes. Aficionados of match racing had long awaited the organization of one-design regattas. In Britain, the Royal Lymington Cup began life in 1974 under the same title as its American counterpart. The event is held in the western Solent each year and has recently been heavily sponsored.

World-class helmsmen, and they might be dinghy sailors or world-girdling racing yachtsmen, are invited by the organizers of the event to compete against one another in evenly matched yachts of identical size and rig. Races are sailed over an Olympic-style course, the size of which is governed by the class of yacht. Points are awarded to skippers for each race, the maximum number available dependent on the number of competitors participating. Points are scored for a win only, and in recent years the Irish yachtsman Harold Cudmore has had the distinction of winning the event five times. In 1986, he also became the first non-American to win the Congressional Cup match racing series held off California.

During its formative years, the races were sailed in borrowed Contessa 32s, a lightweight cruiser racer built by Jeremy Rogers at his Lymington boatyard. Later, in 1979, the brand-new OOD 34s, built by the same firm, were introduced. The OOD 34 was one of a trio of offshore one-designs that included the OOD 101 built by Copland Boats and the Impala OOD 28, which had mushroomed into the world of yacht racing.

This overhead view gives some idea of the accommodation available in an OOD34 designed by Doug Peterson and built by Jeremy Rogers in Lymington.

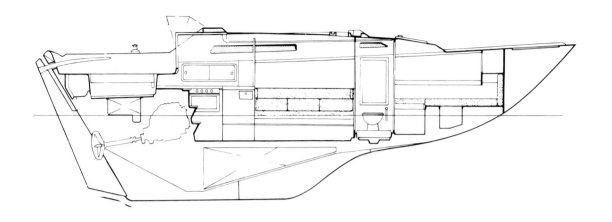

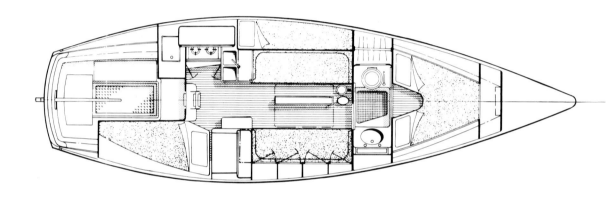

General arrangement and sail
plans showing the Nicholson
31. This popular boat has
largely superceded the highly
successful Nicholson 32
(bottom).

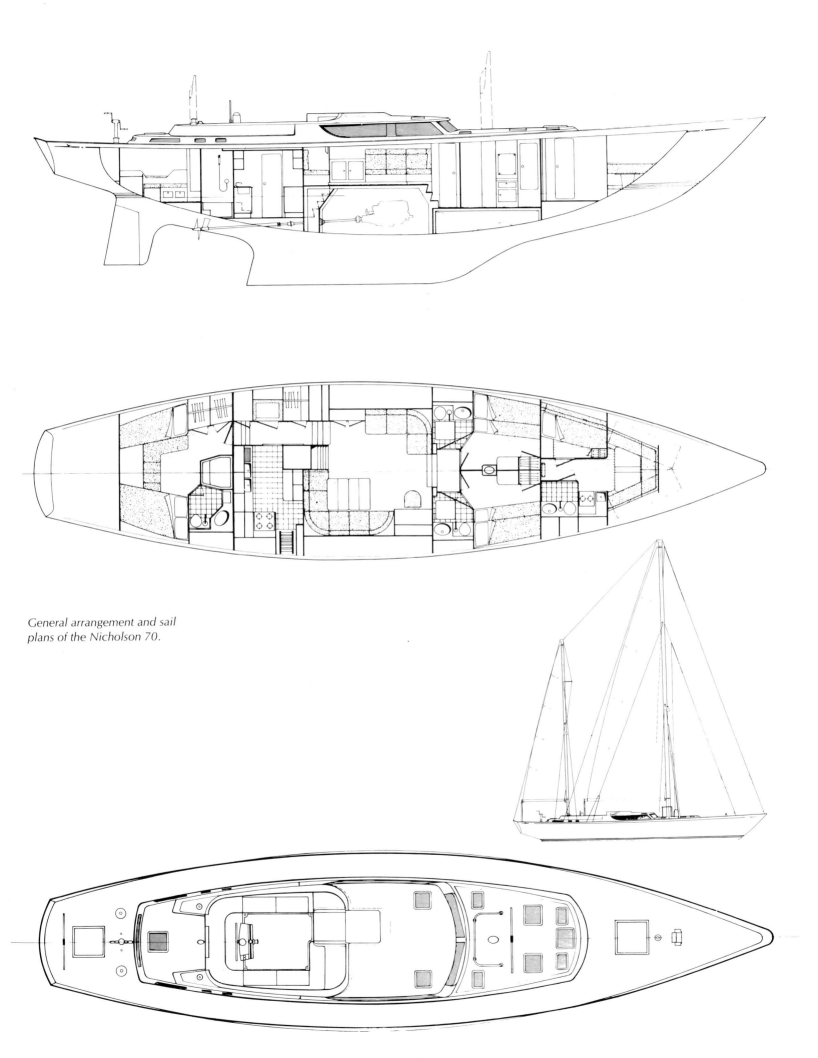

General arrangement and sail plans of the Nicholson 70.

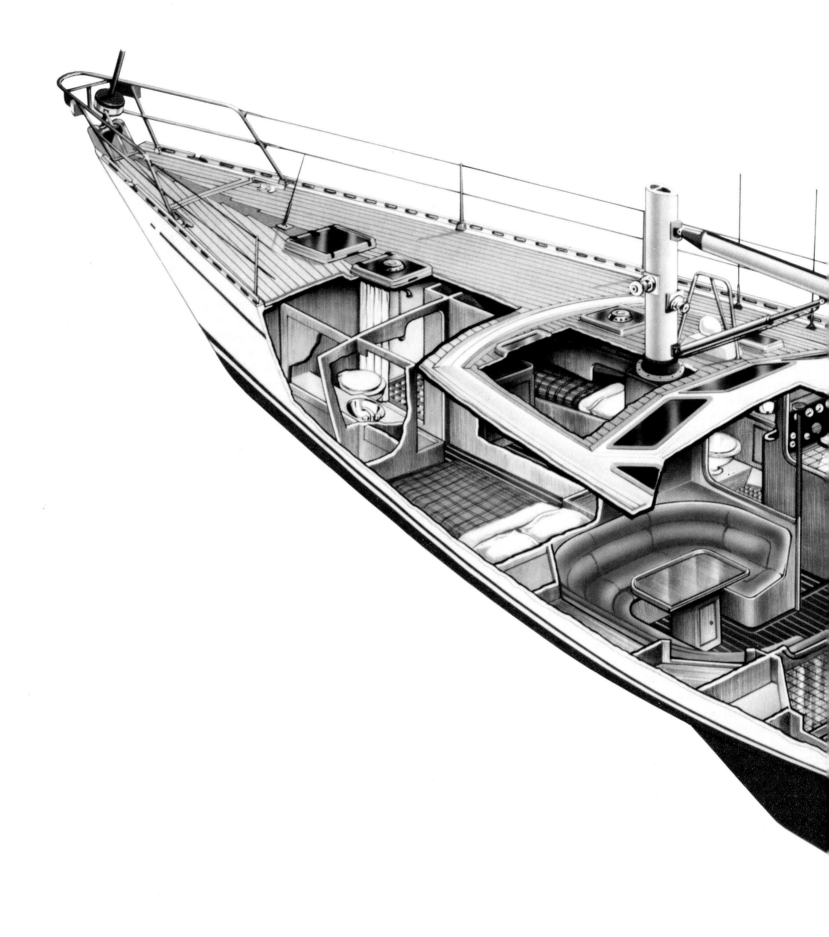

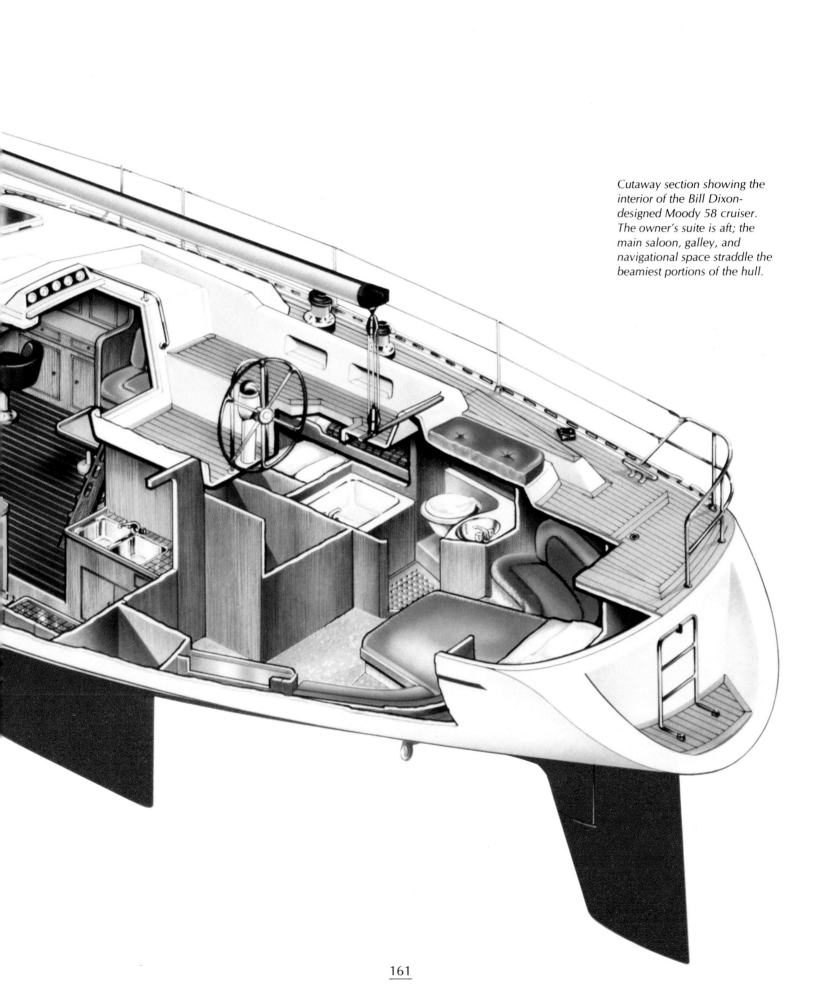

Cutaway section showing the interior of the Bill Dixon-designed Moody 58 cruiser. The owner's suite is aft; the main saloon, galley, and navigational space straddle the beamiest portions of the hull.

This had all come about following a decision made by the Royal Ocean Racing Club (RORC) in December 1977 that its races would no longer be limited to boats measured and rated under the International Offshore Rule (IOR). One-designs would also be allowed to compete. This decision reflected the RORC's awareness of the growing demand from the one-design sector to compete at the local level, a requirement already being met in a small way by the Junior Offshore Group.

Prior to the RORC announcement, Sir Peter Johnson had been appointed chairman of a new group set up to look after the organization and planning of the one-design scene. The three new classes were announced after the Offshore One-Design Conference had scrutinized twenty-six projects by builders in Britain and overseas.

Offshore one-designs were not new, of course. The Scandinavians had long preferred to avoid the IOR setup whenever they could. The Folkboat is typical of earlier one-designs that were very popular in many parts of Europe. The Swedish Albin Ballad, a cruiser/racer similar in concept to the Jeremy Rogers Contessa, still has a huge following in Nordic countries, though by no means as large as when at its peak in the mid seventies. The British SCODs (South Coast One Designs) had been around since the early post-war years and were similar in some respects to the Folkboat. But none of these were ever fast racers. They were, and still are to a large extent, the cruising man's compromise toward racing.

In America, two well-known designers, Dick Carter and Doug Peterson, had by 1978 each designed OODs known as the New York Yacht Club 40—NYYC 40—and the North American 40, both of which are now on the IMS (International Measurement System) standard hulls list.

However, both designs also pander to the IOR, which makes them neither one thing nor the other. In the earlier days of resurgence in the one-design arena, some skeptics argued that such pandering would lead only to a proliferation of designs that were essentially copies of the more successful breed. In the short term, that policy helped to satisfy some of the demand for OODs. In the long term, the need was for an established and proven selection of OODs that yachtsmen might be eager to purchase and enthusiastic to race. Arthur Beiser has said that rating under the IOR is important, but that cruising comforts, interior design, auxiliary machinery, and well-thought-out electrical installations are also strong prerequisites. The hallmark of a good

Joe Cool of Holland (right) and Cetus of Poland in action off Scheveningen during the 1979 half-ton world championships.

cruiser/racer is that it performs both demands with style and success. Of the 400 or so standard hulls listed on the USYRU IMS list updated in 1986, there are dozens of exotic yachts in a variety of lengths to suit almost any demand.

Offshore one-design yachts will probably never enjoy the huge following associated with IOR simply because there are far too many sailors who prefer to compete on a more conservative basis. Preferences for a handicap system far outweigh the one-design rule. This is as true in Europe as it is in the United States. But at least both philosophies are recognized and served.

The rating system currently in use for offshore racing was devised in 1970, when a single rule was established for the rating of ocean racing yachts. Simultaneously, an international administrative system for the management of the rule was also established, known as the Offshore Racing Council, with headquarters in London.

The rule itself and the various formulas used for obtaining the measurement of any given yacht are complex and run to many pages, but, essentially, the rule was devised to replace and to a large extent tidy up a mishmash of rules that had already existed on both sides of the Atlantic but were in many respects poles apart. Among these were the Universal Rule, which produced the J class of the 1930s, the RORC Rule, which was the dominant European rule before the IOR came into being, and the CCA Rule of America, which governed racing in that country. The IOR pulled together all of these separate rules to achieve a single, international handicapping system that would be acceptable to everyone.

Broadly speaking, the IOR has been widely accepted, with the majority of international yacht racing regattas being raced under the auspices of that rule. Designers have excelled in exploring the rule for every possible source of extra speed. Today's racing yachts are just that: go-faster machines, greyhounds of the deep, with beamy hulls and skimming dish underwater sections. The rule has encouraged rapid progress in design, not always, but certainly in most cases, beneficial. Its major virtue is that it is a development rule, encouraging designers to explore their artistic and creative bent as much as their scientific one.

The price of creativity is paid by the boat owner whose primary requisite is a yacht that will provide many of the comforts of home afloat, but who still wishes to race competitively. Until recently, owners of cruiser/racers have been heavily penalized under the IOR rating system. These are mostly production class cruiser/racers, ideally suited to their main purpose in life but good performers nevertheless.

Guy Bernardin's unusual-looking Biscuits Lu, *designed specifically for the 1986 BOC Around Alone Race. Solar panels provide much of the battery charging for electronic equipment.*

Several attempts have been made over the years to produce less stringent rating rules for cruiser/racers, which, in effect, require fewer measurements to be taken. The Channel Handicap and the Scandicap rules are examples. Their accuracy in practice, however, has often been questioned, producing a continued demand for a rating system that would fairly rate any yacht of acknowledged design by producing the best engineering estimates of the speed potential of the yacht when well sailed and equipped.

In America, this need had long been recognized, and in a mandate issued by the USYRU in 1976 the ball was set rolling to find an agreeable method of measurement that would fairly rate the cruiser/racer alongside its IOR counterpart. A system was developed, revised, refined, and finally adopted by the ORC at a meeting in November 1985. Known as the International Measurement System (IMS), it considers and computes essential measurements of the hull to predict the theoretical speed of a boat. Given reasonably accurate information on wind conditions during a race, the IMS, which is a development of the Measurement Handicap System, has proved capable of handicapping yachts with widely different proportions. The 400 or so yacht types listed by the IMS will soon be more accurately rated so that owners will be able to race happily with the prospect of fair placing.

LEVEL RATING

Level-rated racing is probably about as close to one-design as IOR boats can hope to get and is epitomized annually in the hotly contested Ton Cup events organized around the world by the level-rating associations. Any country anxious to hold one of these prestigious regattas is required to bid several years in advance before it acquires host status for any given year.

The first Ton Cup, and still the most sought after and admired trophy in that league, is the One-Ton Cup, first raced for on the Seine at Meulan in 1899. This contest actually came into being the year before when the French yacht *Esterel* had been defeated in a race off Cannes, for the Coupe de France, by the British yacht *Gloria*. The impressive trophy, the One-Ton Cup, is 2 feet 9 inches high and measures 2 feet 2 inches between the handles. It was carved out of a 22-pound block of solid silver by the Paris goldsmith Robert Lenzeler. The cup was paid for with the proceeds of the *Esterel* to Baron Edmund de Rothschild and presented to the Cercle de la Voile de Paris by the owners of the yacht.

Rolly Tasker's magnificent Siska *(right) and Sweden's* Travel *at the start of the* Channel Race off Cowes *in 1979.*

Above: Gumboots, *designed*
by Peterson for Jeremy Rogers.
Below: *The Linge-designed*
Gambling, *a high-performance*
cruiser/racer. Right: *Albin*
Ballad yachts, popular
Scandinavian cruiser/racer
one-designs, start the Gotland
Runt Race in Sweden.

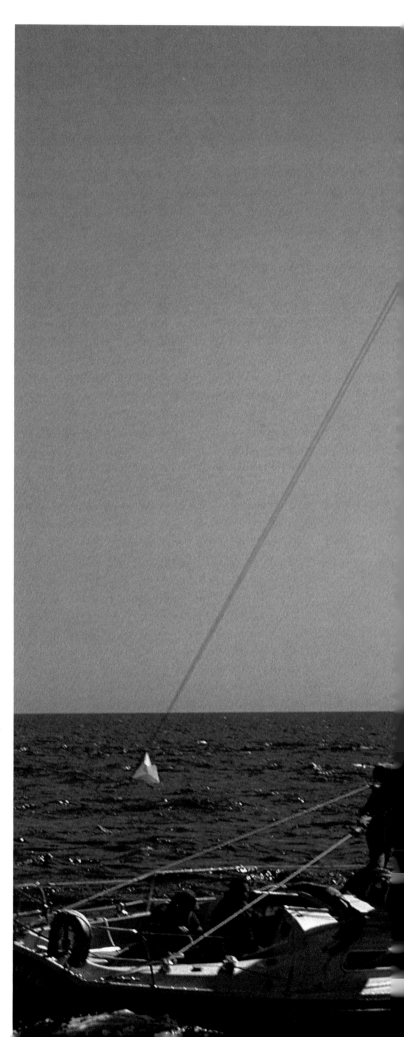

Above: Biscuits Lu. Below:
The French entry AR
Bigouden, *designed by
Bernard Nivelt and Michel
Joubert, won the world
half-ton championships at
Sandhamn in 1980. Opposite:
With the recent relaxation
of the rules concerning
advertising in yacht racing,
sights like this will become
more familiar on the great
racing circuits of the world.*

In the first race on the Seine, the British challenger *Vectis* from the Isle of Wight was beaten by the French defender *Belouga*. Both craft were day boats with fixed keels, rated at one ton or less under the French tonnage rule of 1892. The cup has been raced for on and off ever since. The competitors had to conform to the international 6-meter dimensions until 1965, when new rules were adopted for a combined inshore and offshore regatta for yachts of 22 feet rating under the RORC rules of the time. When the IOR was implemented in 1970, the new rating became 27.5 feet.

From that time onward, the One-Ton Cup series quickly established itself as one of the most important and popular events of the yachting calender, being raced each year in a different location. These events were usually well attended, but the winners, particularly in the early part of the regatta's contemporary history, tended to come from the host nation.

This host-winning tendency was momentarily interrupted in 1976, when the regatta was held off Marseilles, just a few miles from the Côte d'Azur, where the first duel between England and France had been fought some 78 years previously.

The year 1976 marked a significant turning point in the history of the One-Ton Cup, and not only because the regatta was eventually won by the defending country, America. Seventeen nations, the largest turnout since the modern competition had begun in 1965, took part and entered 43 yachts. Among them were two boats entered by New Zealand and designed by a relative newcomer, Bruce Farr. His *Jiminy Cricket* and a new *45 deg South* (another yacht, a half tonner, had cleaned up at Le Havre the previous year) gave an impressive performance on the first day of racing in exhilarating conditions. Both of these yachts displayed Farr's antipodean background and experience in racing and designing the Auckland Harbor skiffs, which came in 12-foot and 18-foot sizes but carried immense amounts of sail and were considered some of the fastest monohull sailboats in the world. Farr's wide sterns and skimming dish hulls were to have a dramatic effect on the yacht designer's art in the ensuing years. The weather on the Rade de Marseille did not hold, however, and in the remainder of a light air series, America's less extreme *Resolute Salmon* became the top-scoring yacht.

Apart from poor attendance at the event the following year, held again in Auckland, support for the competitive one tonner has appreciated rapidly around the world. Simultaneously, classes for smaller "tonners" began to evolve, and there are now Ton Cup championships for just about every level of rating that one might think of. Today, these classes are the mini-ton, quarter, half, three quarter, one, and two ton. At one stage there was even an eight-ton class, but, needless to say, it hardly got a toehold.

Under the present system of rating, ton-class yachts are also eligible, with very minor changes made to suit whichever rating certificate they might need to exhibit, to race in conventional IOR handicap races.

Toward the latter part of the 1980s, ocean racing had become a way of life for a great many people around the world. The sport had long since passed the stage of development it was going through in the mid sixties and early seventies, having grown out of a fledgling of the 1930s. Its rapid expansion from the mid seventies onward was largely due to sponsorship, both seen and subliminal, which had helped to establish some of the greatest sailing events the world will ever see.

By and large, ocean racing's recent history has followed a fairly logical path, growing steadily outward in a kind of circular fashion from hubs of activity in Europe, North America, and Australasia. Just about every conceivable type of ocean race has been established: short, long, and longer for fully crewed, shorthanded, and single-handed racing. In between the larger international regattas, such as SORC, Admiral's Cup, Whitbread World Race, BOC Challenge, the yachting calender is crammed with national events. Some of these also draw competitors from other nations as yachtsmen arrive at the end of, or to begin, other races. So there is activity throughout the year. The keenest racing yachtsman can sail competitively for the most part, enjoying two summers in the same year with very few breaks between events for refitting and repairs.

This huge carnival of yachting has been made possible for the most part by the advent, acceptance, and, ultimately, the exploitation of sponsorship. The rules of the game over the years have prohibited outright commercialism, but that will come quickly now that the organizing bodies of the sport have seen fit to reflect and adjust according to demand. There are many arguments for and against sponsorship in sailing, but whatever the pros and cons, it is fairly obvious that if the sport is to continue developing and expanding in the way that it has, a continuous supply of funds is necessary.

Corporate sponsorship for challenging and defending syndicates competing in the America's Cup is necessary to maintain the high level of technology, for research and development, for building and maintenance programs, for operational expenses. Few of the individuals in the private sector who are interested in the sport have the necessary surplus funds to invest. Although organized by yacht clubs that often have financial assistance from the commercial sector, long-distance ocean racing would have far fewer entries were it not for the individual sponsorship of entrants and their yachts. Level rating and IOR circuit racing, the Ton Cups, Admiral's Cup, Kenwood Cup, the Sardinia Cup, even traditional regattas such as Cowes Week, all benefit directly from sponsorship. These commercial injections help to improve facilities for yachts and crews while creating wider public interest by offering facilities and support to media representatives.

In 1981 at Poole, England, Paul Elvstrom of Denmark sailed the First Evolution/ Beneteau one-tonner, King One, *to victory.*

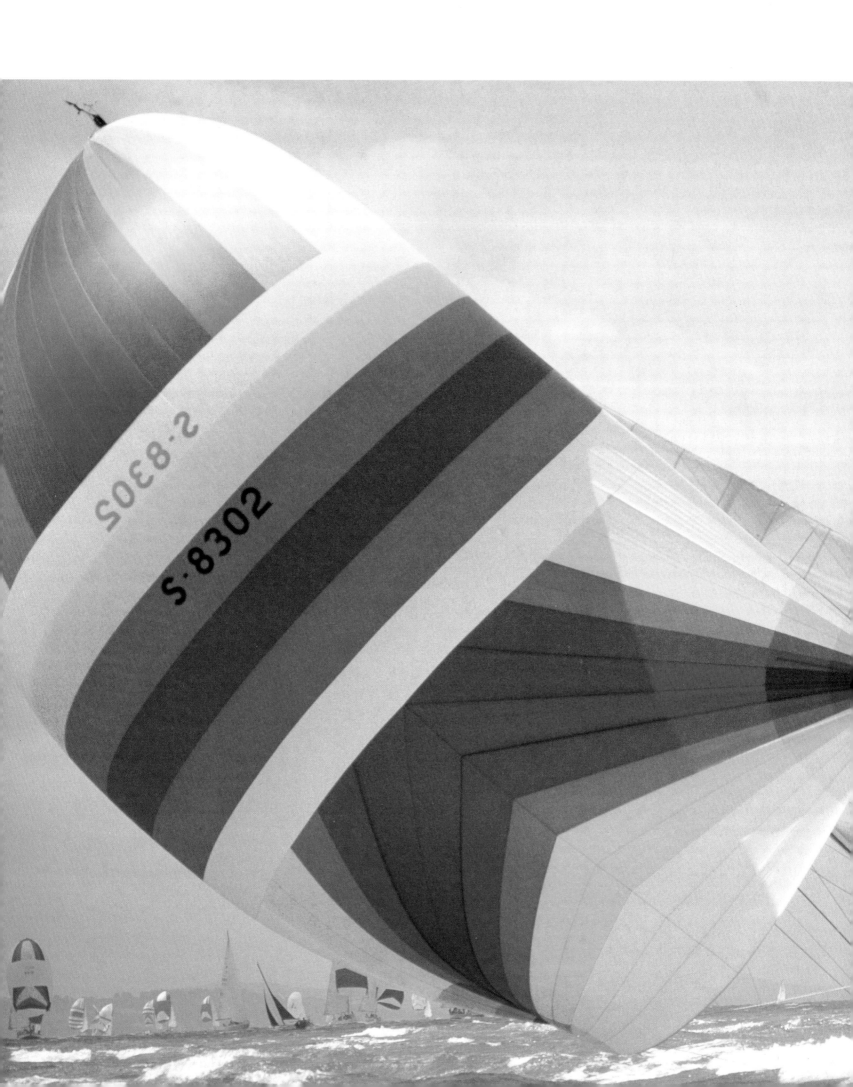

CHAPTER 10

Fast and Furious

Olin Stephens's *Dorade* was the most influential ocean racer of the prewar years. Many attempts were made by designers across the oceans to simulate her lines and, indeed, many yachts produced both before and during the early postwar years by designers like William Fife, Robert Clark, and Laurent Giles bore more than a passing resemblance to the American racer. In Europe, however, conservatism prevailed, so when *Myth of Malham* appeared in 1947 and won the Fastnet Race, she was hailed as a rule cheater. Her owner, creator, and skipper was John Illingworth; Laurent Giles and Partners designed the yacht to his ideas.

Myth of Malham subsequently became the most influential design of the postwar years. Illingworth sailed her from one success to another, convincing those skeptics who had been adamantly against the concept at the outset.

Myth of Malham measured 37 feet 9 inches overall and 33 feet 6 inches on the waterline. Her beam of 9 feet 4 inches gave her a beam to length ratio of 4:1 when the overall length is considered: *Dorade's* ratio was 5:1. Both yachts, however, in considering their waterline length, have identical ratios of 3.6:1 By present-day standards, this is narrow, but when *Myth of Malham* was reaping success over yachts designed in cognizance of earlier theories, Charles Nicholson was insistent that too much beam would be damaging to success. He was proven wrong.

Left: Midnight Sun *yawing heavily during stormy second inshore race of 1979 Admiral's Cup.* Above: Ron Holland's Imp.

Several significant features about *Myth of Malham* helped her to success. The most obvious was her high freeboard, a rule-cheating device that improved her seaworthiness. The RORC Rule of 1947 measured depth (D) in the formula from deck to hull. High freeboard was not seen as a disadvantage even though the rule was later changed. Illingworth moved the mast close to the center of the boat, allowing a larger fore triangle and smaller mainsails set on a short boom. This trend prevails today.

Illingworth's new prodigy was lightly built, allowing the extra ballast to be placed farther down. She had a draft of 7 feet, and this gave her great stiffness and the ability to carry plenty of sail. *Myth of Malham* had chopped-off ends: she was snub-nosed and, in this writer's view, definitely lacking in aesthetic appeal. Nevertheless, Illingworth's creation, certainly a radical departure from convention of the period, was to have a lasting effect.

Ocean racing yachts of that period were still a long way from becoming the stripped-out wide-beamed skimming dishes that they mostly are today. Illingworth's *Mouse of Malham* of 1954 was one of the first departures from tradition, but the idea of hanging the rudder a long way aft of the keel was unacceptable to the racing fraternity. Further, there seemed to be a confusion of ideas between the British and Americans.

Above: *Edward Heath's Sparkman & Stephens-designed* Morning Cloud II. Opposite: *The American team yacht* Carina *of 1971 endures heavy weather in the western Solent. Designed to the CCA rule, she was one of the last of her type.*

The British favored the cutter-style of rig; the Americans, the schooner and yawl. The reasons for this were that the RORC and the CCA in the United States were still a long way from resolving their differences in bringing the racing rules together. In America, the cruiser/racer following was huge. Yachtsmen, their wives, and families enjoyed racing, but enjoyed cruising more. Thus, there was a continual demand for yachts that could accomplish both tasks with a degree of finesse.

In 1955, Olin Stephens drew the lines for the beamy *Finisterre*, a yacht that probably had the greatest effect on the Cruising Club of America. She was 39 feet, a heavy displacement centerboarder giving plenty of accommodation space and shallow draft for cruising. She was first overall in the Bermuda Races of 1956, 1958, and 1960, a record unrivaled by other yachts previously in that race.

With such a long run of success, British and European designers slowly accepted the idea that "beaminess" was not necessarily detrimental to performance. The difference of requirement on both sides of the Atlantic, however, was still a long way from being resolved, but at least progress would be made, for in 1957 an event was begun at Cowes that would eventually focus the attention of the world's greatest designers and spark the imagination of yacht racing organizers worldwide.

The Admiral's Cup series was the brainchild of five senior members of the Royal Ocean Racing Club who were appointed organizers of the event. The idea was mainly to encourage overseas competitors, particularly Americans, to come to British waters every two years to contest the cup—a silver gilt trophy named after Sir Myles Wyatt, then admiral of the RORC. The first event was held in 1957, and since then the series has grown to become the most prestigious and important ocean racing regatta to be held anywhere. In the beginning, two nations, each with three yachts comprising a team, participated. By the late 1980s, the numbers of competing nations had risen to the high teens, with as many as 57 yachts taking part in one year.

The series consists of five races: three raced around inshore courses in the Solent and Christchurch bay areas, and two offshore races. One of these follows a course across the Channel to the French coast and back. The final race is always the Fastnet, in which the Admiral's Cup yachts race as a separate class.

The various national three-boat teams are chosen following a summer of selection trials that, in effect, are normal ocean races in the yachting calendar in which those hopeful for selection compete. European countries often send

Wa Wa Too III, *designed by German Frers, Jr., was built for Fernando Nabuco of Brazil for the 1973 Admiral's Cup.*

Left: *France's* Coyote *(left) and New Zealand's* Epic *hammer it out in Christchurch Bay.*

Above: *Australia's 1985 Admiral's Cup team boat,* Challenge III.

their best yachts to England to participate in the early RORC races in order that they may adjust to local conditions. It is also an opportunity for everyone to gauge the strength of the opposition before racing begins in earnest.

Only five countries took part in the formative years: Britain, which won the first and second matches; America, which took the cup in 1961; France; Sweden; and Holland. Australia joined in the fun in 1965 with Germany and Ireland but went home empty-handed after the British had retrieved the trophy from the Americans. Not to be outdone, the Australians made a second appearance in 1967, along with Denmark, France, Germany, Holland, Ireland, Sweden, and America. The Aussies were successful and walked away with a 104-point lead over their nearest rivals.

After being knocked so heavily, it took the British two more years to recover, despite a new fleet of yachts being launched for the selection trials. Among them was one of the great names in modern ocean racing, Arthur Slater. Crippled in a motor-racing accident some years previously, he was determined to see the cup returned to England. His Sparkman & Stephens–designed *Prospect of Whitby* joined *Phantom* and David Johnson's *Casse Tête III.* The United States was back again with a powerful team that included the two larger yachts *Carina* and *Palawan* and a design by a relative newcomer to the field, Dick Carter's *Red Rooster.*

Carter, a Yale graduate from New England, was one of the first of a new breed of young designers to take ocean racing by the ears and give it a good shake. Later he was to become instrumental in persuading the RORC, the CCA, and the North American Yacht Racing Union to come together and agree to a new international rating rule. He had the assistance of a firm ally in Olin Stephens, who shared Carter's views. But it is ironic that after the IOR was adopted, Carter became one of its firmest critics.

Rabbit was Carter's first attempt at designing a world-beating ocean racer. She was an early "split keeler"; that is, with a fin keel and spade rudder hung well aft. Pure prejudice had outlawed earlier attempts by Van de Stadt, Illingworth, and others to gain acceptance for this idea. Despite the fact that fin and skeg arrangements went as far back as the turn of the century for some yachts, few people would budge away from the convention of long, deep keels with a rudder hung on the trailing edge.

In 1965, *Rabbit,* which had barely been completed by her builders, Frans Maas of Breskens, was firstly disqualified in the Harwich-Hook of Holland race in which she had been eleventh to finish out of 107 starters. As the season progressed, however, this 32-foot low rater, medium-light displacement hull gradually improved her performance, doing well at the first rejuvenated One-Ton Cup at Le Havre, winning the Royal Yacht Squadron's 150th anniversary race, and finally going on to win the Fastnet.

Carter became a prominent force in modern yacht design. *Tina,* a beautifully elegant and deep-bodied racer with swept-back keel, was followed by *Rabbit II,* which the designer sailed in the 1967 Admiral's Cup for America. He was back again in 1969 with *Red Rooster,* which he called "the ultimate RORC rule boat." This 42 footer was a floating test bed for Carter's experiments; her swing keel, which could vary the yacht's draft from 2 feet 9 inches to 9 feet was her most potent weapon. While the Admiral's Cup fleet sailed dutifully around the Solent, competing with the tides instead of one another, Carter upped the plate and went searching for the shallows. *Rooster* scored the highest individual points of any yacht in that year's eleven-team series and romped home in the Fastnet Race, moving the American team from third to first place ahead of the Australians and British.

By now the ocean racing yachting arena was set for a major shake-up, and not just because of the introduction of the IOR in 1970. Nearly all of the great designers of the last decade, and there are many of them, began to emerge from the cockpits of yachts they had learned to sail in, or had themselves designed and built in their own backyards.

The IOR permitted no possibility of compromise. Dick Carter watched as swing keelers and center-boarders incurred massive penalties under the new rule. He did, however, enjoy success with the one-tonner *Ydra,* which won the 1973 world championship in the hands of German sailmaker Hans Beilken. *Ydra* had an easily driven, compact hull and was the first one-tonner to shake off any remaining cobwebs of the RORC/CCA Rule. She was an enormous influence on the up-and-coming new generation of designers like Doug Peterson and Ron Holland. *Ydra's* win at Porto Cervo also marked the end of Dick Carter's one-ton winning streak, which had begun in 1966.

Opposite and above: *General arrangements and sail plan of* Lutine.

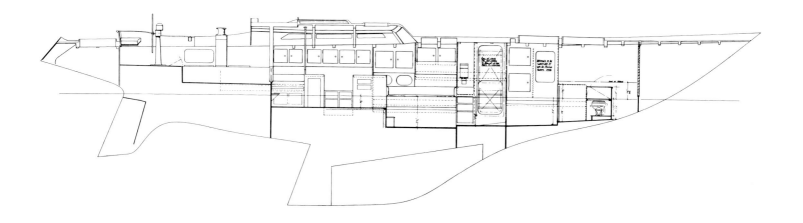

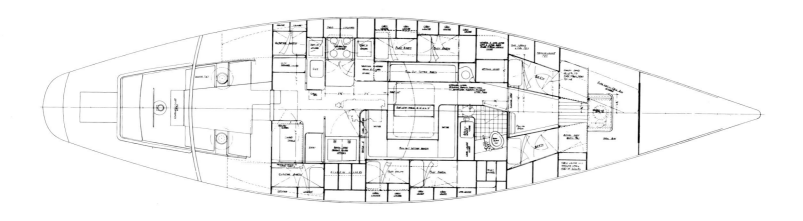

Following pages: *Lloyd's of London commissioned the first of the new C&N 55-footers and named her* Lutine, *replacing an earlier yacht also named after the famous Lloyd's bell. The new yacht had a glass-fiber hull molded by Halmatic; others soon followed her successful path, including the 1973 British Admiral's Cup team yacht,* Quailo III.

Opposite: *The Jeremy Rogers*
Eclipse, *seen here in the 1979
Round the Island Race, was a
Contessa 39 designed by Doug
Peterson and became top
points scorer in the disastrous
Fastnet Race that year.* Above:
Revolution, *designed by Jean-
Marie Finot, racing for France
in the 1973 Admiral's Cup.*

The year 1971 was a significant turning point in the fortunes of the Admiral's Cup and, indeed, yacht racing as a whole. With the IOR still very much in its infancy, an across-the-board boating boom taking place on both sides of the Atlantic, in Europe, and in Australia, yacht racing had begun to attract more than a passing interest in the media.

In Britain, an unwitting government had introduced legislation that banned tobacco advertising from television screens. Tobacco companies had huge promotional budgets to spend—and where better to spend them than on sport? In particular, where better to spend them than on sailing? Alfred Dunhill and Company was already involved with minor sponsorship of dinghy racing, and early in 1971 it was announced that the same company would support the Admiral's Cup series by arranging special facilities for the press and helping with the general administration of the event. It had grown considerably since its inception. It was held at Cowes, right in the middle of the famous Cowes Week Regatta, which, as every English newspaper was aware, was frequented often by the rich and famous and certain members of the royal family.

Naturally, there were cries of disapproval from certain sectors of the fraternity. Yachting was a fresh-air sport, a healthy outdoor activity that should not be associated with the social evil of cigarette smoking. These critics were usually also the very people who were quick to attack the daily press for not carrying enough coverage of sailing events. Simultaneously, whenever more than two inches of coverage reached the sports pages of newspapers, the same critics were there to point out the inaccuracies of reports. It was no wonder the majority of newspapers and their reporters shied away from yachting and gathered at the racetrack.

The exploits of long-distance sailors such as Chichester, Rose, Knox-Johnston, and others had by this time also created something of a public demand for more news of yachting. Another major contributor to this demand was the then prime minister of England, Edward Heath, who in 1971 captained his team to victory in the Admiral's Cup while sailing *Morning Cloud*. Heath, who had progressed from dinghy sailing to a formidable ocean racing opponent by winning the Sydney-Hobart Race in 1969, somehow managed to fulfill all of his political duties and win races at the same time. There can be little doubt that his racing campaigns in the various *Morning Clouds* did much to help publicize both the Admiral's Cup and sailing as a whole.

It was during these years that a young Argentinian by the name of German Frers was busy setting up his own design office, having completed a three-year stint with Sparkman & Stephens on Madison Avenue. Frers's father had long since set up a boatbuilding company in the homeland, and when the time came for German to leave New York with his young bride, an uncertain future awaited him. He need not have worried; during his time with S&S in New York, he had made many contacts, and in his last two years in that city, he had managed to produce the designs for several yachts while working out of his apartment.

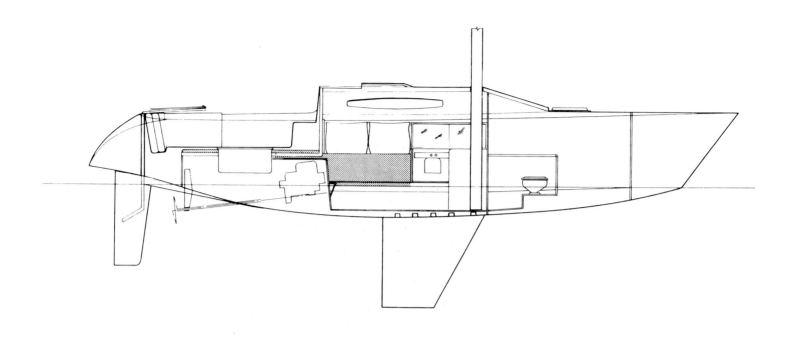

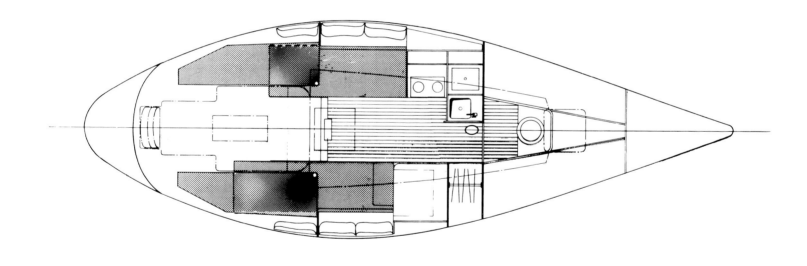

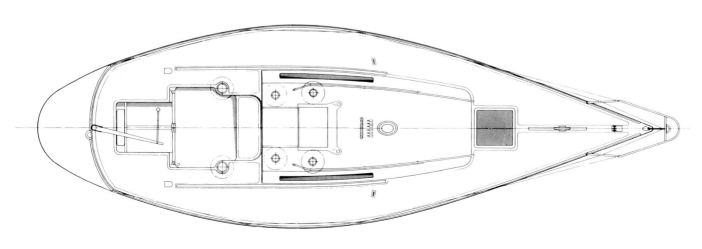

General arrangements and sail plan of a Nicholson half-tonner designed by Ron Holland and based on the yacht Golden Delicious.

SCARAMOUCHE

Scaramouche, *a Frers-designed lightweight with generous sail area, had good light airs potential.*

His fellow yachting aficionados back home in Argentina rallied to the drawing board, and in 1971, Frers, Jr., visited England for the Admiral's Cup with *Matrero*. By the 1973 series, Frers had four yachts competing, including the huge and powerful *Wa Wa Too III*, owned by Fernando Nabuco of Brazil.

Edward Heath was also back with the varnished *Morning Cloud*. The team that year also included a big 55-foot yacht called *Quailo III*. This is a Camper & Nicholson–built cruiser/racer, a development of the first of the type, *Lutine*, which had made her debut from the Gosport yard eighteen months earlier. *Quailo III*, beautiful though she is, was no match for the Brazilian entry *Saga*, which took line honors in that year's Fastnet Race.

The Australians had arrived early in the summer with Syd Fischer's *Ragamuffin* and the Bob Miller (later Ben Lexcen) *Apollo II* and *Ginkgo*, which was to do so well. No one had bargained for Germany, however, which arrived with three potentially powerful yachts designed by Dick Carter and S&S. They were *Saudade*, *Carina III*, and Hans Otto Schumann's *Rubin*.

In the Channel Race, *Saudade* managed a Class 1 first and a fourth in the cup positions. She went on to win both of the following inshore races, her teammates putting up equally surprising performances. Thirty-one points separated Germany from Australia and Britain by the time the Fastnet started. Although *Quailo III* and the Carter-designed *Frigate* managed good final positions, Edward Heath had dropped to the thirty-first position. Germany had a decisive victory.

Their win in this series gave new hope to other European countries as well as to those farther afield, and among the newcomers were Canada, New Zealand, Poland, Japan, Hong Kong, and Singapore.

While Palmer Johnson were building *Wa Wa Too* in Wisconsin, Chuck Kirsch was so taken with the lines that he ordered one the same. In 1974, the German Frers *Scaramouche* won every race in the Onion Patch series. At 54 feet, she rated very low, and during the 1973 SORC series, her rating had been protested several times. Frers claimed that a bigger rig for the yacht enabling her to carry more sail would be beneficial. *Recluta* was another Frers boat that gave a respectable performance in the 1973 Admiral's Cup. Ted Turner's *Tenacious*, which competed in the 1975 series for the USA, was a near sistership to the Argentinian yacht.

In 1979, the Fastnet Race was decimated by a freak storm. Fifteen yachtsmen lost their lives in the worst weather in yachting history. The Australians won the Admiral's Cup with *Ragamuffin*, *Impetuous*, and the Ed Dubois-designed *Police Car* and proved finally that they were probably more used to the severe conditions that prevailed than many of the other countries involved. The surprises were that Hong Kong was third, with Italy and Argentina following close behind. Britain was out of the running after a disastrous navigational error made by Ernest Juer's Frers-designed *Blizzard* in one of the inshore races.

Blizzard epitomized the Frers panache for designing

Another Frers masterpiece,
Bumblebee 3, *raced for*
Australia in the Admiral's
Cup of 1975.

large, elegant, and powerful yachts. A development of this became the Swan 51, a fast and accommodating cruiser/racer production yacht. German Frers was now an established force to be reckoned with. Success piled upon success; inquiries for larger boats began to follow.

His first was a light weather 63 footer called *Il Moro di Venezia*, designed in 1976. *Bumblebee,* for John Kahlbeter, came after and was as close to the 70-foot maximum rating as the IOR allowed. Four more big ones in the mold of *Bumblebee* were built, the last being for Dutchman Cornelis van Reitschoten for his entry in the Whitbread Round-the-World Race of 1982.

The early 1970s were formative years for Frers; by the end of the decade, he and two other young designers had become established legends in yacht racing design. German Frers, Ron Holland, and Doug Peterson had between them produced some of the most exciting boats ever conceived.

Holland is a New Zealander from Auckland, where he

began sailing at a very early age. When he finished school he became apprenticed to a local boatbuilder, and in his last year he and other apprentices designed a 26-foot light displacement cruiser. Four more followed in the next two years. Built of kauri pine, they were cheap and fast. Holland's introduction to the world of big boat racing in America might not have come about had it not been for the interest of one of New Zealand's top naval architects, John Spencer, who introduced Holland to George Kiscaddon, who was in New Zealand to commission a big new schooner.

Spencer's new boat for Kiscaddon was so radical that a 25-foot model of it was built and test sailed with Holland on board. The big version was to be 70 feet overall with only an 11-foot beam. Kiscaddon invited the young Kiwi to stay in the United States and help tune the model while John Spencer finished the drawings for the real version.

In America, Holland met Gary Mull (who designed Tom Blackaller's radical *USA*). After he had seen some of Hol-

Ragamuffin, *launched in 1968.*
Her Bob Miller-designed team
mates, Apollo *and* Ginkgo,
were four years younger.

land's drawings, Mull offered the youngster a job. Mull got the commission for *Improbable,* and hearing that the yacht was to be built of wood, Ron Holland persuaded the owner, Skip Allen, to have it built in New Zealand. It was the same yard in which Holland had served his apprenticeship, and for the next two years he stayed with the yacht, sailing with it in the SORC and the Admiral's Cup.

Holland moved on to spend time with a production yacht builder in Florida. However, while he learned much about the techniques required, his mind was set on designing his own boats. *Eygthene* was the result of years of painstaking thought and hours of spare-time labor spent building the boat with his brother-in-law, Gary Carlin (who later established the famous builders' yard Kiwi Boats in Florida). The yacht was entered for the North American Quarter-Ton Championships and won. Next port of call, Weymouth, England, where the world championships for that class of level rater were being held. Holland's yacht won again.

He was in Europe. He had a winner. It was 1973. Soon, his next yacht, *Golden Apple,* was creating a stir. She was a one tonner, built of wood by the South Coast Boatyard in Cork. The same year, Douglas Peterson had a winner with *Ganbare* in the One-Ton World's Cup in Sardinia. Had Holland remained in America instead of bringing *Eygthene* over for the quarter-ton championships, Peterson might have been asked to design the yacht that was eventually drawn by the New Zealander and christened *Golden Apple.*

Holland and Peterson had been pals for some years. Peterson grew up on the California coastline and was introduced to sailing in much the same way that Holland had been in New Zealand. Holland got to crew on an Alden-designed ketch called *Aloha* in the Auckland to Sydney race when he was 15 years old. When Peterson was the same age, he was racing offshore too, and with that sort of background, it was perhaps inevitable that the paths of the two youngsters would cross before long. They did;

Above: *Australia's* Love & War *in action on the Solent in 1975.* Left: *France's* Revolution. Opposite: *At the helm of* More Opposition, *Robin Knox-Johnston coaxes another tenth of a knot out of the yacht as she heads for a line honors and handicap win in the 1976 Cervantes Trophy Race.*

Opposite: Ragamuffin.
Right: *Albert Buell's German
1973 Admiral's Cup racer
Saudade was an Olin Stephens
wonder boat.*

aboard George Kiscaddon's *Spirit,* the John Spencer maxi schooner whose model trials had first helped Holland to America. Peterson was hired as a replacement crew aboard the yacht in 1964 for the passage back to the United States.

From that time on, Peterson and Holland were virtually inseparable, although Peterson put in many more hours of sea time aboard some of the fastest ocean greyhounds of the time, including the legendary *Stormvogel* and *Ticonderoga.* After being drafted to Japan and Vietnam, where he spent time on a jungle river-boat, Peterson eventually caught up with his old pal Holland aboard another of Kiscaddon's yachts, called *New World.* With Holland was Bill Green, Walter Greene, of multihull fame, and a Japanese designer, Toshio Kihara. The long hours of watchkeeping aboard Kiscaddon's yacht were spent in earnest discussion. Ideas abounded. Peterson was encouraged to call Dick Carter, who offered employment in Massachusetts.

Peterson's family was dismayed at the prospect of losing a member to the East Coast. Funds became available through Peterson's grandmother, and *Ganbare* was built. Compared with other one tonners, it looked a little odd, which its designer says forced him to call in Bill Green, Holland, and Gary Carlin to help him sail it in the North American One-Ton Championship off San Diego. Bill Green says that he was called in with the other two to help Peterson finish building the boat, which they then all raced in and won the event with. That same year in Sardinia, *Ganbare* was second to Carter's *Ydra* in the One-Ton World Championships.

Ganbare was smaller and lighter than anything seen before. She was more easily driven than other IOR yachts of her class. She had a U-shaped bow and a pintail stern that allowed her to point higher and sail through the sea rather than hobbyhorse over it. Observers at the cup event that year knew that Peterson had something special, and by 1974 he had proved it by designing the One-Ton winner *Gumboots* for Jeremy Rogers.

Gumboots was the first glass-fiber design to win the cup. The 1975 winner, *Pied Piper,* built for and sailed by Ted Turner, was in the same mold, but, at 14,000 pounds, both yachts were 2,000 pounds heavier than Peterson's proto-type, *Ganbare. Gumboots* measured 35 feet 6 inches over-all with a waterline length of 29 feet 6 inches and a beam of 11 feet 5 inches. Her draft is 6 feet 4 inches and she carried a sail area of 542 square feet. The length to beam ratio was now little more than 2.5:1, and with her flat underbody and thin streamlined plate keel, she was vastly different to anything produced in the 1930s, 1940s, or 1960s.

At one stage, Holland and Peterson might have worked together, but the American wanted to return to his native Pasadena, while the New Zealander was happily endeavor-ing to settle in Europe. Sparkman & Stephens were still the designers many traditionalists turned to, but the youngsters were making waves. Peterson produced a string of success-ful yachts, each one a subtle variation on the preceding one. Some, like *Yeoman XX* for Robin Aisher, Seymour Sinnett's *Williwaw,* and John McCarthy's three-quarter-ton-ner *Solent Saracen,* were world beaters.

Jeremy Rogers, whose boatyard at Lymington, England, was one of the most successful in turning out production craft with a pedigree of racing success, joined with Peterson to produce *Moonshine*, top-scoring Admiral's Cupper of 1977. It became the Contessa 43. Two years later, *Eclipse*, commissioned by Rogers and Bill Green, became the top-scoring yacht in the 1979 series, although the Rogers-built, Peterson-designed OOD 34s suffered badly in the decimated Fastnet fleet.

Ron Holland was simultaneously producing a flock of yachts to meet demand following the success of *Golden Apple* and *Golden Delicious*, a Camper & Nicholson 33 production boat that won the 1975 Fastnet Race and was second in the Three-Quarter-Ton World's in Norway while being steered by the Bagnall twins, Richard and Harvey. A gaggle of other yachts was launched the same year: *Irish Mist*, *Katsou*, and *Golden Dazy*. After the 1976 One-Ton World's in Marseilles, Holland sat down and drew the lines for *Imp*, which in 1977 became the top points scorer in the Admiral's Cup and was second to *Eclipse* in the series held two years later. *Imp* was a departure from Holland's norm of a tightly tucked-in stern. Bruce Farr's influence with *45 deg South* was beginning to have effect. Before her first Admiral's Cup, owner Dave Allen had entered the yacht for the SORC series, and she was a runaway success.

Marionette, *Big Apple*, and *Regardless* are all yachts of the late seventies that were equally successful. Out of *Marionette* and *Big Apple* was born another Swan production cruiser/racer, the 441. *Imp* became a Swan 39, while *Regardless* was used as the yardstick for the Swan 412. Much of Holland's work today is involved with production yachts and the larger IOR maxi racers. He worked with Laurie Davidson of *Waverider* fame on the New Zealand America's Cup challengers for 1986–87 and may become more involved with 12 meters if time allows in the future.

By the end of the 1970s, Holland and Peterson, Bruce Farr, and Carter had been joined by others. Laurie Davidson, Ed Dubois, Valicelli, Joubert and Nivelt, Jean-Marie Finot and Briand, Rob Humphreys and Castro, Vrolijk of *Diva* fame were among the twenty top yacht designers in the world. Some of them were still struggling with occasional success, also to become legends. That Peterson and Holland and Farr could be counted alongside the Nicholsons and the Herreshoffs, there was little doubt. Some of their boats were not successful—you cannot have winners all the time—but these designers were essentially a product of a changing era, lucky enough to be in the right place at the right time. Others have produced good boats, some winners and some losers, but not much that has changed radically from the designs already produced by the Ron Hollands and Doug Petersons of this world.

Australia's Impetuous *leads Hong Kong's* La Pantera *in the second inshore race of the 1979 Admiral's Cup off Cowes.*

CHAPTER 11

Men and Yachts Against the Sea

The single-handed world-girdling exploits of the late Sir Francis Chichester in *Gipspy Moth IV* and Sir Alec Rose in his 36-foot ketch *Lively Lady* caught the imagination of the public during the late 1960s.

Chichester was the latter-day adventurer, a flier and a sailor, an instigator, with Blondie Hasler, of the single-handed transatlantic race. He was never one to sit still and watch the world pass by. He inspired the "Drake" in everyone. He also had backing for his exploits in the form of an extremely successful family chart-and-map-publishing business. Alec Rose (now Sir Alec) was a greengrocer. He and his wife kept a small, fresh fruit and vegetable shop in Southsea. He kept his 1948 Indian-teak-built cruising ketch nearby and liked to sail in the waters of the Solent.

His reasons for wanting to sail off around the world alone were quite simple. He had always wanted to do it. With Rose it wasn't a case of living for every moment he could go afloat. Yacht racing, as such, was not on his curriculum. When he first set off from Portsmouth in 1966, his *Lively Lady* was involved in a night collision with an unidentified freighter off Ushant. Rose returned dejectedly to Portsmouth, where he repaired the ketch and began to prepare for another attempt the following year.

Left: *Perils in the Southern Ocean: icebergs and the freezing cold.* Above: *The sea: single-handed sailors have battled against these elements for decades.*

Like a magnet, Cape Horn draws solo sailors and world-girdling yachtsmen. Tales concern its occasional sighting, but many have sailed around it through devastating storms, never to sight the jutting promontory.

On July 16, 1967, he set off from Langstone Harbor surrounded by a small armada of well-wishers. Seven weeks prior to this date, Sir Francis Chichester had sailed the 54-foot *Gypsy Moth IV* in to a tumultous welcome in Plymouth—the first man to sail around the world single-handed with only one stop. A few days before Rose departed, Chichester received the ultimate accolade from Her Majesty the Queen at a public ceremony on the banks of the Thames at Greenwich. Solo fever raged throughout England; the public was hooked, and the newspapers went to town on the greengrocer's departure.

The heavy seas Rose encountered on the first leg of his voyage to Melbourne cost him dearly in terms of equipment and the effort needed to repair broken gear while under way. Setting sail once more, he was forced to put into Bluff, New Zealand, to effect further repairs to the rigging and self-steering gear. From here he continued to Portsmouth, nonstop, via Cape Horn, to a massive welcome arranged on the beaches of Southsea on July 4, 1968. A knighthood quickly followed as well as a book that was translated into many languages. Lesser men might have ridden out the rest of their lives on the waves of publicity that followed his triumphant return, but Sir Alec and Lady Rose continued to open the little greengrocer's shop on Osborne Road.

The next logical step would be to sail all the way around the world without stopping. Several men, some with commercial backing and some without, were now preparing to follow in the wake of the two intrepid pioneers. Commander Bill King had secured the backing of one of Britain's largest daily newspapers, and in France, Bernard Moitessier was reportedly planning his voyage eagerly.

The English Sunday newspaper *The Observer* had sometime previously established a lead in yachting circles by sponsoring the quadrennial single-handed race across the Atlantic—le Transat, as the French came to call it—which Chichester had begun with his friends at the Royal Western Yacht Club in Plymouth. *The Observer*'s main competitor, *The Sunday Times,* made a fresh appraisal of all that was happening in the world of yachting and, on the suggestion of two of its staff, Murray Sayle and Ron Hall, announced a single-handed race around the world.

The Golden Globe Race offered an enticing £5,000 for the fastest time and a further prize for the first yacht to finish. The announcement came in March 1968, while Rose was still at sea. A formal, written entry was not required, but the conditions called for all competitors to begin their voyages between June 1 and October 31 of the same year! Not what anyone would call a great deal of time for a thorough preparation for such a formidable voyage, though anyone who started was in the race whether he liked it or not.

In spite of this time factor, nine people managed to sail in time to qualify for the prize. Among them were names that were later to become synonymous with spectacular ocean racing achievements. There were Chay Blyth and John Ridgway, the two paratroopers who rowed across the Atlantic in a Yorkshire dory in 1966 named *English Rose II* and who were now going their own separate ways in production-built glass-fiber sloops. There were Frenchman Louis Fougeron and Italian Alex Carozzo, Bill King with *Galway Blazer*, Nigel Tetley in the Music for Pleasure–sponsored trimaran *Victress*, and Donald Crowhurst, an electronics specialist, in his trimaran *Teignmouth Electron*.

No officials scrutinized the contestants' craft to see if they met even basic safety requirements. Though all of the yachtsmen were experienced seafarers, the hurried departure, as much as anything, contributed to their eventual withdrawal and to the tragic disappearance of Donald Crowhurst.

It should be remembered that these men had no precedent for what they were about to undertake. Many single-handed sailors had gone before on long ocean cruises in yachts that were perfectly suited to that cause, but now it was more than a cruise. Yachts would begin to be pushed harder; the inspiration a pot of gold at the end of a long hard slog. This was to be no mooch around the Solent in a force 6.

Blyth put into Port Elizabeth with broken gear and eventually sailed home on a cruise with his wife. Ridgway stopped at Brazil for repairs, so he went out. Bill King's strange-looking *Galway Blazer* was knocked down, and he could continue to port only under jury rig. The Italian, in the 66-foot ketch *Gancia Americano*, put into Lisbon after falling ill. Louis Fougeron put into St. Helena with damage to his gaff cutter. Nigel Tetley, an ex Royal Navy frigate commander, looked at one time to be a serious contender for the main prize. His was the first trimaran to round the cape that all sailors fear and respect most—the Horn. But closer to home, *Victress* began to take water and eventually broke up.

The intrepid commander was forced to take to his life raft while still 800 miles west of the Spanish coast. He was spotted by an aircraft of the U.S. Air Force after it had detected distress signals from Tetley's emergency radio. Luckily, he was picked up without injury the same day as the aircraft sighting by the tanker *Pampero*. Until the wrecking, *Victress* had certainly been the fastest of the world girdlers, having crossed her outward track after only 179 days.

Donald Crowhurst had set off from Teignmouth in another trimaran only nine hours before the deadline set by *The Sunday Times*. Crowhurst's plans to get away early were beset with problems, and he sailed with gear and equipment still unfitted and stores piled all over the saloon. But he made good progress toward the South Atlantic, and regular radio messages to *The Sunday Times* showed that he was probably making a better average speed than Tetley. Since Tetley was also in communication with the paper, news of Crowhurst's achievements may well have spurred him to push *Victress* too hard, which in turn would have contributed to her eventual breakup.

Crowhurst pressed on. Radio contact with him never seemed to falter. The positions he radioed home plotted his

Mountainous seas in the Roaring Forties and the Southern Ocean present a constant danger to those who sail on them. In these southern latitudes, huge seas have taken their toll on yachts and men.

Chay Blyth sails British Steel *triumphantly up the Solent on August 6, 1971, to a truly royal welcome.*

course across the Southern Ocean and round the Horn so that by the summer of 1969 it looked as if he might well be in with a chance for the main prize. But on June 23, Crowhurst made his last entry in the log and disappeared. Crowhurst's "round-the-world" voyage was simply one gigantic hoax.

He had set sail sure enough, but a month after leaving Teignmouth he had decided that he could not continue with the circumnavigation in a yacht that was so ill prepared. He set a course immediately for the South Atlantic, where he cruised erratically. At one stage, he landed secretly on a beach on the Argentine coast to carry out repairs.

Setting sail once more, he went as far south as the Falkland Islands and then began his tortuous voyage toward home. Crowhurst was on a psychological downhill slide. At home he had left a wife and children and heavy financial commitments that might result in losing his home, and now he had to face the public and explain how he had not sailed around the world.

On July 10, 1969, the freighter *Picardy,* captained by Richard Box and sailing in flat, calm seas near the Azores, spotted *Teignmouth Electron* drifting helplessly, her sails set, and no visible sign of life on board. A lifeboat was lowered from the ship, and a boarding party under the command of the chief officer was sent to investigate. The party met with an eerie experience. The yacht seemed to be in good condition, no smashed equipment and an apparently lived-in saloon. But there was no sign of any crew. The yacht was deserted. Later examination of the vessel's logbooks revealed the complete hoax. It was thought that Crowhurst might have suffered hallucinations. His schizoid personality shattered, he had almost certainly jumped overboard.

The Frenchman Bernard Moitessier left Plymouth on August 22, 1968, with the intention of sailing around the world, returning to England briefly to comply with the rules of the race, and then departing once again on another voyage. His 39-foot 6-inch steel-hulled ketch *Joshua,* named after one of his favorite writers of the sea, Joshua Slocum, was ideally suited to a voyage of this nature. Moitessier sailed south into the Roaring Forties and on south of Tasmania and New Zealand to the Horn, which he had already seen on a previous voyage.

Joshua was not equipped with a radio, but the Frenchman's method of passing messages to ships that came close seemed to work well enough. He was well round the Horn and heading north to Europe when, on March 18, he catapulted this message onto the bridge of a passing merchantman: "The Horn was rounded on 5th February. I am continuing nonstop toward the Pacific Islands because I am happy at sea, and perhaps also to save my soul." That was the last anyone saw or heard of Moitessier for three months, until he sailed into Tahiti on June 21, 1969. *Joshua* was storm battered, having twice suffered knockdowns in the Indian Ocean and again in the Pacific. His following was great in France, and people were dismayed to hear of their countryman's retirement from the race. The prize had been within his grasp. What could he possibly have been thinking of?

Bernard Moitessier had spent 301 days at sea and had covered a record 37,455 miles, of which 29,000 miles were spent sailing in the Roaring Forties. All of these statistics constituted new achievements in shorthanded sailing, but Moitessier was unrepentant about ditching the race; the thought of a competition at sea was, he said, "grotesque."

So now only one man was left to complete the voyage. Robin Knox-Johnston, then 30 years old, left Falmouth in Cornwall on June 14, 1968, in a vessel that was one of the smallest to take part and, at the time, was thought to be the least likely to complete the voyage, let alone stand a

Above: *Alec Rose arrives off Southsea in* Lively Lady *in June 1968.* Right: *The junk-rigged* Galway Blazer, *built for a nonstop solo circumnavigation attempt by Bill King, seen here preparing for the 1976 OSTAR.*

chance of winning any prizes.

Suhaili was a Bermudan-rigged ketch, built of solid teak, with masts and spars of Kashmiri pine. She was constructed by local Indian craftsmen using the same tools that had built warships in the same Bombay yard over a hundred years before. At the time of her building in 1964, Knox-Johnston was serving as an officer in the British Merchant Navy with the British India Company. When *Suhaili* was completed, he and his brother Christopher and another crewman sailed the boat home to England by way of Cape Town.

Her design was that of a double-ended Bermudan ketch, measuring a mere 28 feet on the waterline. Overall she was 44 feet, including the bowsprit. She was beamy at just over 11 feet and had a draft of nearly 6 feet—a dumpy little boat that could not by any means be classed as an ocean greyhound. In fact, her owner, having decided to take part in the Golden Globe Race, initially looked for a sponsor for a larger, more suitable craft. He was unsuccessful in that quest, but after the 74-day voyage from Cape Town to Gravesend in 1965, Robin had no doubt about the seaworthiness of *Suhaili* or of his ability to sail her on a longer voyage. For the race, the wooden mizzen was replaced with a lighter alloy one and a home-built self-steering gear erected. By the time he was ready to go, the yacht was fully provisioned and as equipped as she would ever be.

Robin's departure went virtually unnoticed save for the paper that had sponsored the race. I recall thinking at the time, after seeing a photograph of *Suhaili* leaving the River Fal, that she looked like the kind of craft that would probably make it in one piece, even if it took half a lifetime. She was sturdy, slow, but pretty. She had a look about her that exuded confidence in an ability to climb mountains.

Two months after his departure, *Suhaili* was hit by huge waves in the Roaring Forties and knocked over. The cabin was awash with water, books, charts, and provisions all wallowing in confusion. The coach roof was damaged, and large cracks had appeared where the sides had shifted away from the deck. The homemade self-steering gear mounted alongside the mizzen was hopelessly damaged. In the days that followed, Knox-Johnston suffered the wrath of five gales over a period of ten days. No sooner had one finished than another started.

But Robin, not one to give up easily, drove on to New Zealand, where he anchored off Otago to carry out repairs, now much needed if he were to complete the course. Though he touched bottom and spoke to a few people, he received no outside assistance and, since he had not put into a port, the rules of the race had not been infringed. He set sail again in November and headed for the dreaded Horn. He rounded it on January 17, 1969, sighting it briefly

Yachts and multihulls of all shapes and sizes line up in Plymouth's Milbay docks before the start of a transatlantic single-handed race.

Left: *Robin Knox-Johnston, the first man to sail single-handed nonstop around the world.* Above: *Swedish solo yachtsman Sven Lundin squeezes into the hutchlike accommodation of* Bris. Opposite: *Chay Blyth.*

from 8 miles off until a rain squall blotted out the dark outline. By the time the squall was over, the Horn was well aft of the beam and Knox-Johnston had set course for the Channel.

This course took him almost up the middle of the South Atlantic and then into the Northern Hemisphere. He sailed north of the Azores and far to the west of his outward track on a beeline for the Bishop Rock Light south of the Scilly Isles. The month was April. The weather in the Western Approaches was typically damp and blustery from the southwest when a tiny monoplane swooped out of the gray skies to welcome *Suhaili* home. Rust streaks from the chainplates, an oil-smudged bow, and gray sails to match the sky were evidence of the little boat's epic voyage.

At 1525 local time on April 22, Robin Knox-Johnston sailed across the finish line. When a customs officer asked him from which port he had come, the lone sailor replied heartily, "Falmouth!" Afterward, he was taken ashore in the Royal Cornwall Yacht Club tender. He had been at sea for 313 days, but the doctor in attendance pronounced him the sanest man he had met for a long time. The Golden Globe and the prize money were Robin's. He was awarded the

MBE, wrote a best-selling book, and settled down to a new life ashore running boatyards, a marina, and building and sailing fast ocean racing multihulls.

This aggressive and determined sailor would have sailed around the world single-handed with or without the entice-ment of the prize; indeed, he donated the money to a fund set up for the dependents of Donald Crowhurst.

Some people often wonder why lone sailors who have made it around the world are not totally demented by the time they step back onto dry land. It is true that some have had problems in adjusting once they were ashore again. In Knox-Johnston's case, I am sure that his years at sea as a professional seaman, where many hours can be spent alone keeping watch in spite of the fact that a ship is a hive of human activity, had conditioned him for the long and lonely days he was to endure. Chichester was an adventur-er who already had a long history of solo experiences, both on the water and in the air. Chay Blyth, who was shortly to set off on another epic voyage, was once a sergeant in the Parachute Regiment who knew what self-discipline meant and practiced it. Eric Tabarly, the Frenchman who was to become the idol of his countrymen, was a naval lieutenant

when he first hit the headlines. The odd ones out are people like Sir Alec Rose, who was 58 years old when he set out in *Lively Lady*. Most of his life had been spent in daily contact with the public, so what was it that enabled him to keep his balance, while someone like Tetley, another man with a service career, eventually gave in to the pressures? In Sir Alec's case, it was probably the fact that in the years that he had thought about and planned the voyage, he had already sailed many of the miles in his mind. Being out there alone, passing the hours by talking with the man in the moon or discussing the weather with the local albatross, was as natural to him as passing the time of day with one of his regular customers at the shop in Southsea.

By now, of course, there did not seem to be much left to achieve in the way of single-handed sailing. The Observer Single-Handed Transatlantic Race (OSTAR) was well established, the fleets of competitors growing with each event. Since 1945, some 126 single-handed sailing exploits of all types had been logged. The layperson could easily be forgiven for thinking there was nothing left to conquer. For the dedicated yachtsman, however, single-handed sailing, creating new records, attempting the impossible and suc-

ceeding were the spurs that drove a seemingly endless list of people to sea on a voyage of adventure.

For centuries, sailing ships and yachts had followed the most natural routes of wind in their voyages around the world. Long-distance windward sailing had always been considered an impractical and risky business; imagine beating into mountainous head seas and gales for thousands of miles.

For one man, at least, that thought may not have been too daunting. The Scottish ex-paratrooper Chay Blyth was not altogether unfamiliar with huge seas and, having once attempted to circumnavigate the world in entirely the wrong type of craft, he was now embarked upon a mission to sail around it the wrong way—from west to east, single-handed and nonstop!

Blyth was no fool. He knew that he would need a vessel much stronger than anything that had already completed a circumnavigation in the conventional manner. A member of Parliament whom Blyth had approached pointed him in the direction of the British Steel Corporation, which thought Blyth's plans a great idea and offered to sponsor them from their promotional budget. The yacht was named *British Steel* after the material used for her construction to a design by Robert Clark. She was built by Philip & Son Ltd. of Dartmouth. The British Steel Corporation loaned technical advisers who ensured that only the best grades of steel were used.

When completed and launched in mid August 1970, *British Steel* was probably the most ideal yacht for any long-distance ocean crossing. Measuring 59 feet overall with a beam of 12 feet 10 inches and a draft of 8 feet, she had a low, flush deck with a collision bulkhead forward that could be sealed with a watertight door if the need arose. She had a fin keel, which at the time was thought most unsuitable by traditionalists for a craft of this nature, while her rudder was hung at the after end of the waterline. Clark had specified tiller steering instead of the wheel normally found on a yacht of this size, and this was linked to a self-steering vane. *British Steel*'s cockpit was tiny, designed to keep her skipper in one place in the event of heavy weather and huge seas crashing across the deck. Her rig was that of a Bermudan ketch, kitted out with a wardrobe of sails that could easily be handled by one man under the worst conditions.

Blyth's impending voyage was not a race so much as an attempt to prove that a west-east passage was possible, though naturally he wanted to complete it in the fastest possible time. He chose the River Hamble near Southampton as his departure and arrival point and on October 18, 1970, set off across the starting line at the mouth of that famous river. Following the route of many other adventurers, Blyth and *British Steel* were soon out of the English Channel and heading for the Equator. Sixty days after leaving the Hamble the yacht was approaching the southeastern tip of Argentina where, on December 23, Blyth was met by the Royal Navy ice-patrol ship HMS *Endurance*, which exchanged mail and fresh food with the lone sailor. On Christmas Eve, light winds guided the yacht through a calm sea around the tip of Cape Horn, but by nightfall a fresh wind had struck up from the southwest. While people were celebrating Christmas Day in comfortable sitting rooms in the Northern Hemisphere or sat on the beaches of Bondi in the Southern, Blyth was slogging through a force 9 gale that had whipped the sea into a boiling caldron, smashed his self-steering gear, and split open his head. He hove to for a while and then pressed on into a northwesterly, which was now pushing him toward the icebergs farther south.

For days this pattern of vicious, bitterly cold weather hammered away relentlessly at the big ketch. When the wind moderated, *British Steel* sailed on in thick fog, sometimes averaging 7 to 8 knots. Toward the end of February, Blyth passed the South Island of New Zealand. His self-steering gear still broken, he was spending up to twenty-four hours at the tiller, catnapping whenever he could. But there were still thousands of miles to go. In the spring, off southwestern Australia, Blyth radioed the British Steel Corporation an ETA (estimated time of arrival) for the Hamble River of August 7. Was this another of the jovial Scotsman's wee jokes?

No one who hasn't done it can imagine what it must have been like out there in those vast wasteful oceans, battling with gales for day after day, mile after mile. The man's stamina, like the hull of his ship, must have been iron-founded to withstand so many hours at the helm in that tiny cockpit. On one occasion the boat was swamped with such a massive weight of green water that Blyth had time to wonder whether she would ever lift herself out of it.

One tends to carry a mental picture of the long-distance sailor sliding down the sides of huge seas, the sunlight glinting through each wave crest as it breaks, marveling at the hugeness and the wonder of it all. From Blyth's accounts of the voyage, one has the impression that he spent every day in those southern latitudes working just to stay alive. There was no letup from the interminable gales and mountainous seas. From Cape Horn to the southern Indian Ocean took three months: 90 days. It would have been very tempting to run for the shelter and comfort of the dry land of Western Australia rather than face another month of gales before the Cape of Good Hope could be rounded.

Blyth kept going. There was no stopping him, it seemed, or his pounding ketch. Once round the southern tip of Africa, he picked up the southerly trade winds, a pile of messages, and some Champagne from a South African warship. The self-steering was still out of action, and the tiller had been broken on the 2,000-mile haul from Australia to Africa. He was now steering with a jury tiller, sleeping underneath it and never giving up the challenge of trying to make the yacht steer herself.

At the end of July, HMS *Ark Royal* hove in sight and made a wide circle around *British Steel*. The end was near. A week later, in the Channel, the minesweeper HMS *Glasserton* assumed the big carrier's escort duties. But Blyth was ahead of his ETA, so the convoy slowed in order to arrive at the Hamble at the end of Cowes Week, where a huge reception awaited him at the Royal Southern Yacht Club. *British Steel* entered the Solent on August 6, 1971, to a welcome from hundreds of pleasure craft. Blyth received a right royal welcome, and he too was later awarded the OBE. One of the most remarkable and most noticeable features of Blyth's homecoming was that *British Steel* looked far from battered, with her paintwork almost as bright and gleaming as it had been the day she was launched. Cosmetics aside, the yacht's great shape was due to the thoroughness of Robert Clark's work on the drawing board.

This wasn't the end of Blyth's adventures, nor Knox-Johnston's. Both men became inextricably involved in the sport of yacht racing. Their exploits are now legend, and so are the yachts they sailed.

Passing the Horn—and catching sight of it—is cause enough for celebration. The crew of Condor *dress appropriately as the Horn recedes astern during the 1977-78 Whitbread World Race.*

CHAPTER 12

The Jester and the Giants

On June 11, 1960, four British skippers and a Frenchman pioneered what has since become a cult in yacht racing. The OSTAR—the Observer Single-Handed Trans-Atlantic Race—is no longer sponsored by *The Observer*, the newspaper under whose banner it grew and expanded. In its history, it has attracted by far the largest number of competitors in vessels of many different shapes and sizes from all corners of the world. The sailors who compete are a breed whose dreams and ambitions could be fulfilled only in solitary ocean crossings.

In the year of its inception, the tiny fleet consisted of Blondie Hasler of "Cockleshell Hero" fame, who sailed the tiny 25-foot junk-rigged Folkboat called *Jester;* Francis Chichester in *Gipsy Moth III,* a 37-foot wooden-hulled Bermudan cutter; David Lewis in a 28-foot Vertue-class sloop named *Cardinal Vertue;* and Val Howells in *Eira,* another 25-foot Folkboat. Jean Lacombe had started the race but returned to Plymouth for repairs and reached America 74 days later. Francis Chichester won the race in just over 40 days. A week later, Hasler arrived in *Jester,* but the other two took considerably longer because they both had had to call at ports in Ireland and Bermuda to effect repairs.

Left: Flyer *was constructed of aluminum with closely spaced transverse frames and additional longitudinals to stiffen her.* Above: *Simon le Bon manning one of the coffee grinders aboard his yacht Drum of England.*

Opposite: Jester, *built and rigged by H.G. "Blondie" Hasler in 1953, was the smallest of the seven entrants in the first OSTAR race in 1960. Above: Michael Richey has sailed* Jester *in every single-handed transatlantic race since 1964, attending to the simple Chinese lug rig from his cockpit station.*

Lacombe's efforts to reach America had fired the French with enthusiasm. If the rules said, "any size, any shape, any type," then they would do whatever had to be done to win the prizes. Unwittingly, perhaps, it was this "anything goes" attitude that was later to cause some controversy and aggravation between the British organizers and a handful of French competitors who had become so fanatical in their efforts to win that Hasler's original concept was largely overlooked.

Blondie Hasler, that inimitable designer and planner, was the driving force behind the race. It has often been reported that the introduction of the event stemmed from a wager between Hasler and Francis Chichester. The latter had suggested to the Royal Marines officer that if he could not raise the support of the Royal Western Yacht Club to run the race, then they would both go anyway, the winner collecting the grand sum of half a crown (then about thirty cents).

Both men were accomplished single-handed sailors, and the idea of the race was not to see who could get to the other side first, but "that it should be a sporting event to encourage the development of suitable boats, gear, supplies and technique for single-handed passages under sail. The intention being that the Atlantic Ocean itself, with all its vagaries, should be the real arbiter of success or failure."

Opposite: Rogue Wave.
Above: Alaska Eagle (ex Flyer)
*sets out from Portsmouth
on the first leg of the 1982
world race.* Right: *Hasler's
experiments to perfect the
Chinese lugsail and his
successful crossing of the
Atlantic spawned similar rigs.
John Christian sailed the junk-
rigged Ek Soeki for the 1976
event but was forced to retire.*
Following pages: *The 56-foot
trimaran Fleury Michon,
skippered by Philippe Poupon,
was the first to cross the
Atlantic in 1984.*

Halser and Chichester both felt that ocean racing was becoming far too expensive and beyond the reach of the aspiring sailor whose budget was limited to perhaps a small production cruiser or a home-built craft. People also wanted boats that they could use at other times, for cruising, an ideal much cherished in the United States. Craft built under the strict measurement rules governing the design of pure racing craft would have limited usefulness as family boats. So the only important rule to be considered was that each yacht in the race could be skippered and crewed by only one person.

The rules were quite simple. Entries had to be driven by the force of the wind or the strength of the crew—you could row the Atlantic if you felt so inclined! There were no rules governing the shape, size, or type of boat that could be entered until after the 1976 event, by which time things were beginning to get a little out of hand. Various arguments concerning the safety aspects of such a race appeared in print soon after the race was announced. These arguments have withered somewhat since, but questions

Left: Ocean Spirit, *sailed
by Robin Knox-Johnston and
Leslie Williams, won the 1970
Round Britain Race with a
two-day lead over her nearest
rival.* Above: Lion New
Zealand, *skippered by Peter
Blake, who has competed in
every Whitbread World Race.*
Right: *Naomi James is greeted
off Dartmouth as she sails her*
Express Crusader *home.*

Above: *Canadian Mike Birch skippers some of the fastest multihulls afloat, most of them designed by Nigel Irens.* Right: Condor of Bermuda *arrives off Portsmouth in 1978.*

are still raised about whether it is sensible to race a vessel single-handed over long distances when a proper lookout cannot be kept.

In the ensuing years, the race created national heroes and, perhaps inevitably, brought tragedy. The tiny *Jester* encouraged others to junk their rigs. She is the only yacht to have started in every single event since 1960. The rules encouraged experimental craft, including a number of very successful multihulls like *Gulf Streamer, The Third Turtle, Manureva, Fleury Michon,* and many others. In 1972, Frenchman Jean Yves Terlain entered the largest monohull ever sailed single-handed on any ocean. She was the Dick Carter-designed *Vendredi Treize,* which at 128 feet overall was considered a monster.

Carter's objective, however, was to propel one man across an ocean with the greatest of ease. His solution was simply to make a rig that was manageable and then fit the largest possible hull underneath it. He maintained that a 70 percent efficiency, compared with 95 percent on a regular crewed racer, would be more than sufficient to give an outstanding performance. In that surmise, he was not wrong. *Vendredi Treize* led directly to Carter's Luna rig, which he named and patented after a yacht he designed for an Italian customer using the *Vendredi* concept.

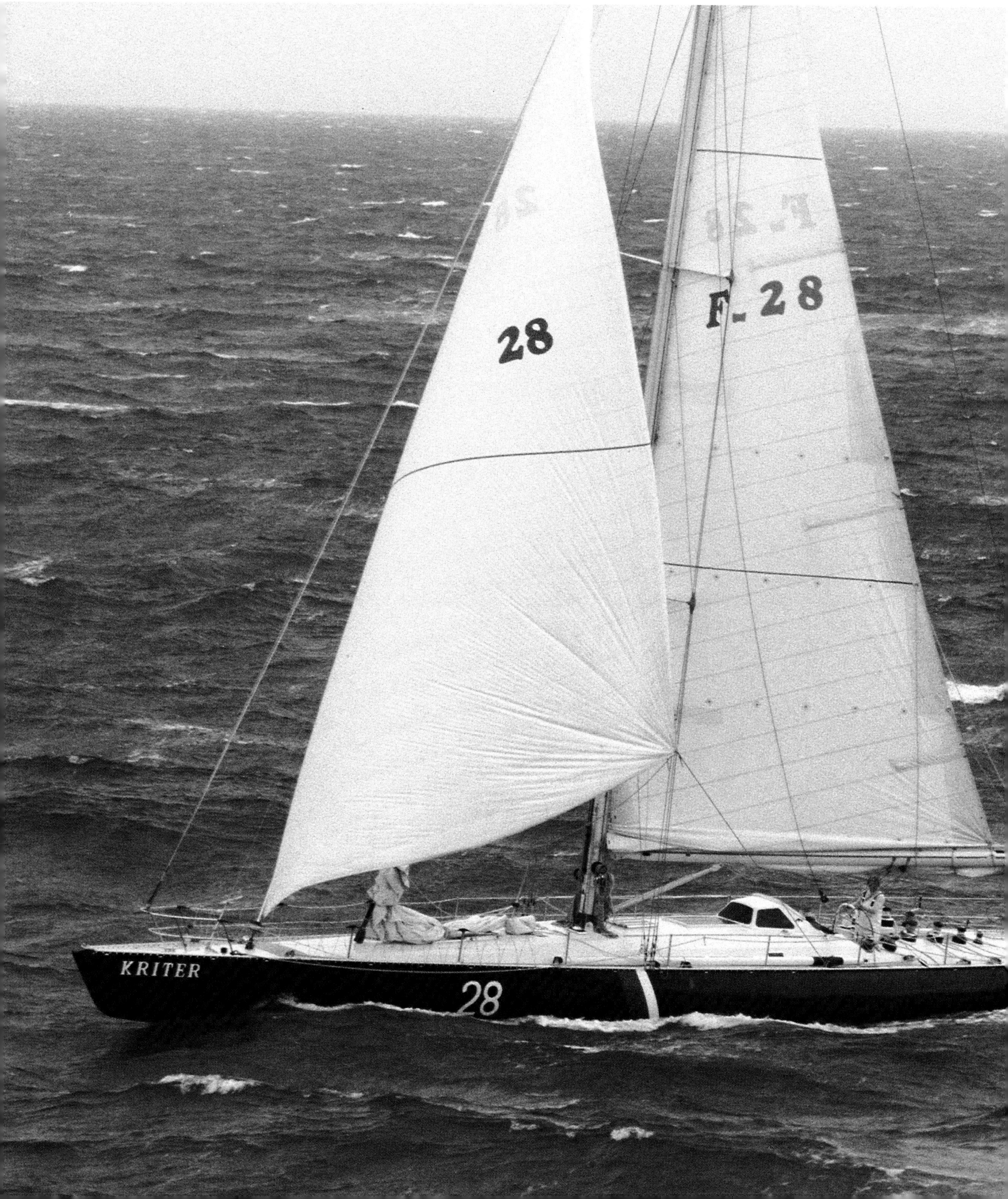
28
F. 28
KRITER
28

Left: *Michel Malinovsky of France sailed the pencil-thin* Kriter *in the 1982* Route du Rhum. Above: *At 236 feet overall,* Club Mediterranée *is the largest sailing vessel to have been sailed single-handed.*

Vendredi Treize was a three-masted staysail schooner sponsored for the event by French filmmaker Claude Lelouch. Terlain was second at the finish behind a relative newcomer to the sport, Frenchman Alain Colas. It was also the year of the multihulls. Eight took part in the race that year. The trimarans came first, third, fifth, and sixth, with Colas setting a new record for the course of 21 days 13 hours at an average speed of 5.8 knots.

Alain Colas was a dedicated yachtsman and a brilliant seaman. One wonders if he was not perhaps just a little too obsessed with winning and in establishing himself as the world's premier single-handed sailor. In 1973, Colas changed the name of his trimaran to *Manureva* in honor of his beautiful fiancée, Teura, and,' as multihulls were not eligible to compete in the first Whitbread Round-the-World Race being staged that year, he set off from St. Malo in France to shadow the fleet.

While the monohulls put in to three compulsory stopovers, Colas broke the voyage only once, in Sydney. He completed the 29,000-mile voyage in 168 days at an average speed of 7.34 knots. Shortly after his return to St. Malo, Colas nearly lost a foot in an accident aboard the yacht, but he arrived with his brother Jean Francois to sail the big trimaran in the 1974 Royal Western/Observer two-man round-Britain race. Colas was now convinced that his

Above: *Eric Tabarly and his crew arrive in* Pen Duick VI *off Portsmouth at the end of the 1978 Whitbread race. Right: Bassin Vaubin in the port of St. Malo, quadrennial starting point for the many varied craft that enter the Route du Rhum.*

winning, had to put into St. John's in Newfoundland with blown-out sails and parted halyards. His repairs took 35 hours, and although he set off again with the intention of being first into Newport, he was pipped at the post by *Pen Duick VI* and an exhausted Tabarly, who had spent four days at the helm without a break. He had, in fact, been without his self-steering gear for 21 of the 24 days it took him to complete the course. Tabarly's radio silence had caught everyone on the hop, but the French supporters were ecstatic. Colas was not. Eighteen hours behind Colas came the Canadian Mike Birch in his 32-foot trimaran *Third Turtle,* creating a new record time for a boat of this size of 24 days 19 hours.

Following the introduction of new regulations regarding the size of entries for the OSTAR in 1976. Frenchman Michel Etevenon decided in December of that year to organize a single-handed race across the Atlantic that would reflect the "creativity of the human exploit." There were to be no restrictions on type, size, or the number of boats allowed to enter, provided that entries met a minimum waterline length of 36 feet. The regulations, such as they were, provided for a freedom of choice in the type vessel most likely to make the Atlantic crossing in the fastest possible time. And, of course, individual sponsorship would be encouraged. The race was organized jointly by the UNCL, Promovoile Guadeloupe, and the French daily newspaper *L'Equipe.*

Thus the Route du Rhum race was born. The course is from St. Malo in Brittany, on the northwest coast of France, to Point-à-Pitre in Guadeloupe, a distance of 4,000 miles. In addition to trophies, the first race in 1978 offered a financial reward of some 500,000 French francs to be shared out among the first six boats to cross the line.

There have now been three of these spectacular events staged from France. It has been heavily subscribed by the multihull yachtsmen since the beginning. A number of interesting monohulls have also competed, but is is sad to note that even a race like this, which tends to encourage multihull development, has cost the lives of some of the best-known exponents of the art. Alain Colas disappeared in 1978 in *Manureva.* Loic Caradec, in the huge 80-foot catamaran *Royale,* was lost in the 1986 event.

GIANTS OF THE OCEAN

The first ever fully crewed race for Class 1 yachts on a course around the world began on September 8, 1973, when a huge 100-year-old cannon was fired by Sir Alec Rose from the battlements of Southsea Castle to signal the start of this historic event. Seventeen yachts from seven countries, ranging in size from 45 feet to 80 feet, were about to pioneer a new era in ocean racing.

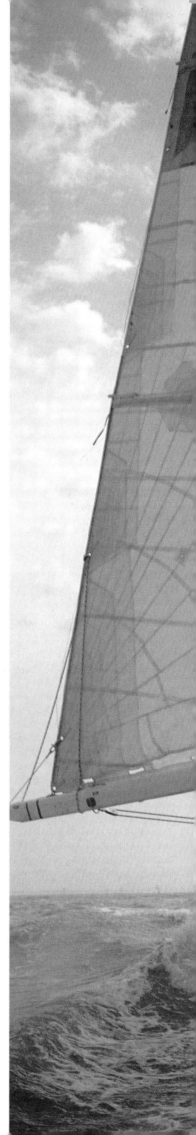

Sistership to UBS Switzerland, Atlantic Privateer *is owned and skippered by Padda Kuttel.*

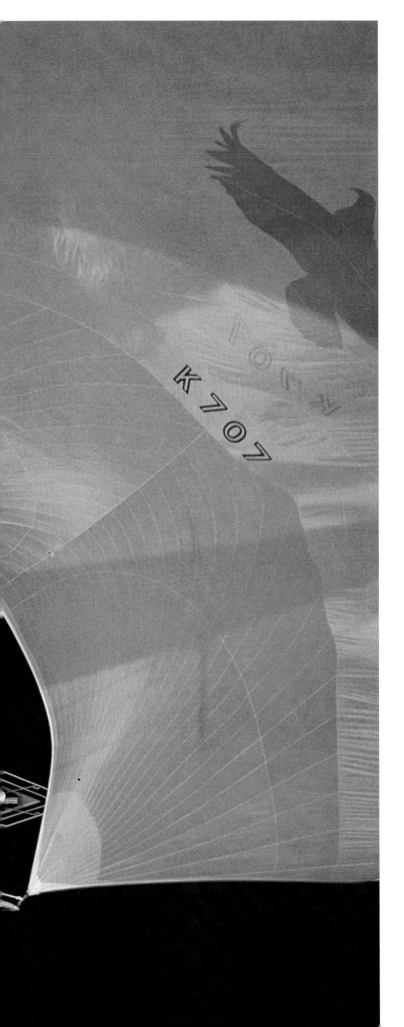

Left: *Seagull's-eye view from the top of* Condor's *98-foot carbon-fiber mast during the 1977 Fastnet.* Above: *Work on* Condor's *hull nears completion. The wooden-hulled boat was cold-molded in mahogany.*

A world-girdling race for fully crewed yachts became inevitable following Robin Knox-Johnston's successful single-handed circumnavigation. Many people in Europe were aware of the inadequate organization behind the Golden Globe race, so it was as much out of need as the pursuance of adventure afloat that two men publicized their ideas for a race for Class 1 yachts. Anthony Churchill and Guy Pearse, both publishers and experienced yachtsmen, knew that they could not organize such a race alone. They turned to the Royal Naval Sailing Association, which has its headquarters in Portsmouth, for assistance. Under the guidance of its full-time race secretary, Captain Dudley Norman, the RNSA had set up a race committee under the chairmanship of Rear-Admiral Otto Steiner in the spring of 1972. Finance was also needed to support a race being organized on such a large geographic scale, and this ultimately came from English brewers, Whitbread.

The excitement that the announcement of this race created was immense, and not just among a few yachtsmen. The general public thronged to the beaches of Southsea and jammed the Solent starting area with an estimated 2,000 spectator craft. There had never been anything like it before. Newspapers and television crews from all over the world gave it unparalleled coverage. It was, indeed, a breathtaking concept.

Opposite: *Entries moored at* HMS Vernon *in Portsmouth at start of Whitbread race.* Above: Condor, *an 80-foot maxi-racer.* Below: United Friendly *(ex GBII). Following pages:* The Royal Navy's Adventure, *a 55-foot C&N glass-fiber entry in the 1973–74 world race, was out of the same mold as* Lutine.

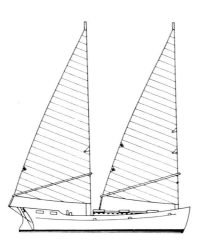

Right: *Sail plan of* Charles Heidsieck. Right below: *Sail plan of a 40-foot Freedom wishbone ketch.* Far right: Charles Heidsieck III, *showing her stretched transom, starting the 1982 Whitbread race.*

Breathtaking too were many of the yachts that competed in this and subsequent races, the most recent of which ended in 1986. In the first race, two major opponents faced each other with formidable craft. Eric Tabarly was racing in the Mauric-designed *Pen Duick VI,* while Chay Blyth sported a huge Airex foam-sandwich construction of 77 feet called *Great Britain II* (the first was Brunel's steamship of the same name).

Great Britain II is arguably one of the finest racing yachts ever to have been built in England and raced under the British flag. The other is the original *Condor of Bermuda* of 1977. *GBII,* as she is affectionately known, was designed by Alan Gurney, who produced from his drawing board one of the fastest maxi-ocean racers ever built, *Windward Passage,* which after seventeen years of more or less continuous racing was retired after the 1987 Sydney-Hobart race. At 77 feet 2 inches, *GBII* is slightly longer than her forebear and was 3 feet 2 inches longer on the waterline at 68 feet 2 inches; but at 18 feet 5 inches, her beam was nearly a foot narrower. *Windward Passage* had a deeper draft by 6 inches at 9 feet 6 inches and was 7,000 pounds heavier

than the British yacht at 80,000 pounds.

These maxi yachts took little regard of the rules of the time, although the CCA of pre-1970 allowed a maximum overall length of 73 feet; hence the reason that *Windward Passage* measured 72 feet 9 inches overall. These maxi yachts were built as potential line honors winners, their owners only interest in being first home regardless of any rating. The IOR introduced a permanent maximum of 70 feet rating under the rule, so yachts designed after that introduction had somewhat more elegant lines at the ends. Nevertheless, the owners of *Windward Passage*, Mark and Ben Johnson, competed favorably against most newcomers for a very long time. In her first season, *Windward Passage* finished first in every race in which she took part. In 1971 she raced from Los Angeles to Honolulu in 9 days, 5 hours, 34 minutes, and 22 seconds, an average speed of 10.02 knots. Her fastest indicated speed was logged at over 20 knots.

Great Britain II has been entered in every Whitbread Round-the-World Race to date, the Parmelia Race, and many other shorter races. She has set many records and has probably clocked more miles under her keel than most ocean racers of similar size—close to 175,000 nautical miles at the last count. Chay Blyth took line honors in the

Above: *Ramon Carlin's magnificent Swan 65 Sayula took overall handicap honors in the 1973–74 Whitbread.* Opposite: King's Legend, *a Swan 65, racing up the English Channel under spinnaker at the end of the 1978 Whitbread race.*

first Whitbread race; the late Rob James skippered her to a new record elapsed time in 1977–78 (while his wife, Naomi, was endeavoring to become the first woman to sail single-handed around the world in *Express Crusader,* ex *Spirit of Cutty Sark,* which Leslie Williams had sailed to fourth place in the 1968 OSTAR), and Blyth raced her again in 1981-82 when Celia Unger took ownership.

The overall handicap winner of 1973–74 was Ramon Carlin's *Sayula,* a production Swan 65, a yacht that seemed to be eminently suited to such long-distance racing despite the fact that she went through one of the worst 360-degree rolls ever recorded.

In 1977–78, while Knox-Johnston, Leslie Williams, and Peter Blake were driving the new Bob Bell *Condor* to line honors, a Dutchman named Cornelis Van Reitschoten, then himself heading for an overall handicap in his first Sparkman & Stephens-designed *Flyer,* was scheming ahead to the next race. He went to German Frers for a new *Flyer* after a visit to Wolter Huisman's boatyard at Vollenhove, where he saw the 76-foot *Helisara* under construction for conductor Herbert von Karajan. This was the first of four boats by Frers that were a development of *Bumblebee,* and Reitschoten was so taken with her lines that he commissioned the new building on the spot.

The hull lines of the two boats were similar, but after that everything changed. Additional framing was added as well as longitudinal framing between the stem and the main frame in way of the mast, to help stiffen the bows. *Burton Cutter,* an aluminium monster 80 footer, had suffered dramatic panting problems in the South Atlantic and more or less as soon as the yacht left Cape Town on the second leg of the race. The Dutchman, with one race under his belt, was taking no chances with his potential winner. Her construction was interesting from the point of view that no structural bulkheads were fitted to the hull—the yacht relied entirely on framing for her strength. The yacht also carried a larger keel, set farther aft than on her sistership; this would help to improve balance by counteracting the enormous weight of sails to be carried in her fo'c'sle.

The outcome of that race is now well documented history. The "Flying Dutchman" won his race, narrowly beating Peter Blake in *Ceramco New Zealand.* Blake's *Cermaco* was something of a comeback for the New Zealand designer Bruce Farr, who had taken a self-imposed layoff from designing IOR boats following near disasters with earlier level-rating yachts like *Red Lion* and *Export Lion,* which had been heavily penalized under the rule. *Ceramco* won the 1980 Sydney-Hobart and was a hot favorite for line honors in the 1981–82 Whitbread race. Farr had also designed the 58-foot Pierre Fehlmann entry, *Disque d'Or,* but neither yacht performed as well as their owners had hoped.

Fehlmann, however, was not disillusioned with Farr's ability and went back to the Kiwi designer for a larger boat along similar lines. *UBS Switzerland* was the result, a rocket of a yacht that not even Frenchman Eric Tabarly could catch in his beautiful-looking *Côte d'Or. UBS* is a powerful machine, designed to save time by giving an

Lion New Zealand, *designed by Bruce Farr.*

246

entire half knot of average speed on a day's run. Over a period, that saving can amount to a large percentage, saving days at the end of a passage rather than hours. Fehlmann failed to get line honors in only one of the four legs of the 1985–86 race but was well ahead on the last leg and surfed into the Solent at 14 to 15 knots.

One other yacht, which nearly didn't compete in this race, or in any other, is worthy of note. Before Robert James lost his life in a boating accident off England's Devon coast, he had intended to sail in the 1985–86 Whitbread race in a custom-designed and built glass-fiber maxi-rater. Colt Cars (GB) Ltd., which had been the sponsors of his successful trimaran, had sponsored the building of the hull. James would never see it completed.

Amid some secrecy, the hull, which had been designed by Ron Holland, was sold and transported to a building shed on the River Hamble at A. H. Moody's boatyard. She would be fitted out under the supervision of one of the world's top ocean racing yachtsmen, Skip Novak, who had nearly beaten Van Reitschoten's early *Flyer* in another Swan production yacht called *King's Legend* in 1978.

Subsequently it was revealed that the new yacht would be named *Drum of England*. The hull had been purchased by an English pop star, Simon le Bon of Duran Duran fame. The yacht was entered for the 1985 Whitbread event, but during the Fastnet Race of that year she lost her keel, turned turtle, and all but sank. There was no loss of life, and the hull was salvaged and towed into Falmouth. In the few weeks that were left before the start of the world race, Novak and his crew and a team of fitters virtually stripped the yacht and rebuilt it. She was on the line off Gillkicker as Dame Naomi James fired the starting cannon from HMS *Glasgow*. I don't think there was a single spectator among the thousands who had gathered along the mist-shrouded shores and in the huge spectator fleet who was not rooting for Le Bon to win. He didn't, but given another 24 hours, he might have.

Whatever the "Flying Dutchman" may have said about not being able to urinate over the stern of a Holland-designed maxi (a design concern not within the scope of this work), there are and probably always will be customers lining up for his yachts. His designs exude a note of surety, of quiet aggressiveness combined with a degree of elegance that others somehow lack.

Condor, *designed by*
Ron Holland.

Afterword

This tapestry of contemporary yachting is only part complete. In fact, it can never be wholly complete or even up to date. Too much has taken place in the past twenty years for one book to cope with. Ten volumes of a similar thickness, sans illustrations, with three columns of text per page in 8-point type might do justice to the subject.

The early years of the seventies spawned a whole new generation of "events" to which yachtsmen have flocked in their thousands. Yacht production, the actual building of new vessels, has increased proportionately, catering not only to the mass leisure market, but in vast quantities for the thoroughbred race market. Hand in hand with this expansion came a whole army of yacht designers endeavoring to satisfy the needs of the serious racing and cruising yachtsmen as well as the whims of those just as serious but often regarded by the establishment as outrageous. Whether attempting to cross the Atlantic in the largest vessel possible for serious single-handing, or the smallest, these sailors who participate have helped to make yachting a more varied, interesting, competitive, and colorful circus in which I, for one, am happy to be involved.

It is probably true to say that, compared with other forms of transportation, the development of sailboats has been painfully slow. The sea is not like a road. Evaluation of new ideas takes time, and years may pass before they are seen to work efficiently and become accepted. Sometimes they are never accepted, especially by other designers.

Once a particular design is accepted on a wide scale, it takes almost as long to change the then current thinking to something new. The IOR, with its continual minor changes, often outlaws good ideas while encouraging the development of others, although the rule as such was never envisaged or established solely for technical advancement despite the fact that it has gone through periods when it appeared to be a development rule.

Looking back over recent years, I can think of a list of yachts as long as my arm that probably should have been included in this work. Intrinsic elegance, however, is not always an arbiter of how well any yacht may perform. By the same token, positive ugliness would have ruled out some others, a number of ULDBs (ultra-light displacement boats) among them. Some designers may feel somewhat miffed that they have been omitted. In particular, there are bound to be many younger designers whose works may well have rated a mention and some no doubt who will feel that what they have designed should have rated more. Perhaps. But time will tell.

Drum *bites hard into a fuming Solent at the start of the 1985 Fastnet Race. A few hours later she turned turtle, her* keel *snapped off. All aboard were rescued, and the yacht was salvaged.*

MAJOR DESIGNERS

Andrieu, Daniel France
Antheor; *Cifraline*; *Indulgence*

Bentall, E. H. England
Jullanar, first real racing yacht in Britain without workboat lines;
Evolution, with first fin keel

Briand, Philippe France
Assisted with Sverige; designed *French Kiss*; *Freelance*; *Passion II*;
Panda; *Esprit D'Equipe*

Hasler

Burgess, Edward USA
Designed *Puritan* and other greats; adapted designs of English Itchen
ferry boats

Burgess, Starling USA
J class America's Cup defenders: *Enterprise*, *Rainbow*, *Ranger*

Cary-Smith, A. USA
First American to design yachts on paper before construction;
Mischief; *Vindex*, first yacht built of iron; small craft and riverboats

Castro

Castro, Tony England
Justine III/IV; *Tsunami*; *Balthazaar*; *Whopper*; *Itzapurla*; *Itzapurlatoo*

Herreshoff

Chance, Britton, Jr. USA
Experienced meter yacht designer; *Chanceggar*, *Intrepid* (with S&S),
Mariner; codesigned *Stars & Stripes*

Cole, Peter Australia
Sail designer; designs cruising boats, including Cole 43s and
Nantuckets; *Steak & Kidney*

Chance

Davidson, Laurie New Zealand
Codesigned 12Ms *KZ-3*, *KZ-5*, and *KZ-27*; IOR yachts

Holland

Farr, Bruce New Zealand
Codesigner *KZ-3*, *KZ-5*, *KZ-7*; *UBS Switzerland* and many other
famous IOR yachts

Fox, Uffa England
All types of sailing and some powered craft; *Avenger*

Giorgetti, Franco Italy
Codesigner of *Italia I*, *Italia II*

Fox

Gurney, Alan USA
Windward Passage; *Great Britain II*

Hollom

Hasler, H. G. "Blondie" England
Devised the Chinese lug "junk" rig for *Jester*; self-steering
equipment; "peanut" rowing dinghy

Herreshoff, Francis USA
Whirlwhind and other great racers of the 1930s to 1950s

Herreshoff, Nathaniel USA
America's Cup defenders: *Vigilant*, *Defender*, *Columbia*, *Reliance*

Irens

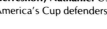

Holland, Ron New Zealand
Famed for IOR craft; *Imp*, a classic, codesigner *KZ-3, KZ-5, KZ-27*

Hollom, David England
Codesigner *Crusader II*; model yacht designs

Howlett, Ian England
12Ms; *Lionheart*; *Victory*; *Crusader I*; half scale model *Kurrewa VI*

Illingworth, J. H. England
Designer of radical ocean racers; *Myth of Malham*

Irens, Nigel England
Lightweight multihulls, including *Vital*; *Apricot*; *Fleurey Michon*

Kirby, Bruce Canada
12M designer of *Canada I*; *Canada II*; laser sailing dinghy

Langan, Bill USA
Designer with Sparkman & Stephens; *Freedom*, modified *Courageous*; *America II*

Lexcen, Ben Australia
Apollo, Ginko; *Ballyhoo*; *Australia II*

Magrini, Giorgio Italy
Formed part of *Italia II* group; designed entries for '87 America's Cup challenge

Mauric, Andre France
Long-distance ocean racing yachts; *Pen Duick VI*

Mull, Gary USA
IOR yachts; 6M; codesigner of *USA*

Murray, Iain Australia
Codesigner of *Kookaburra I, II, III*

Nelson, Bruce USA
IOR yachts, including *Sleeper*; one of the designers of the 12M *Stars & Stripes*

Nicholson, Charles E. England
Designed many of the greatest racing yachts in English history, among them *Endeavour*

Pedrick, David USA
Sparkman & Stephens; worked on design of *Courageous*; *Nirvana*, which holds Fastnet Race record

Peterson, Doug USA
Ganbare; *Gumboots*; *Imp*; *Eclipse*; *Yena*; *Rubin*; *Ragamuffin*; *Moonshine*

Petterson, Pelle Sweden
Sverige; 6Ms; maxi-class cruising yachts

Shuttleworth, John England
Britanny Ferries GB; *Travacrest Seaway*

Lexcen

Murray

Nelson

Pedrick

Shuttleworth

Stadt, E. G. Van de Holland
Racing yachts and luxury craft; *Zeevalk*

Stephens, Olin USA
Designer for Sparkman & Stephens; *Dorade, Stormy Weather*; *Finisterre*; *Vim*; *Columbia, Intrepid*

Valentijn, Johan USA
Sparkman & Stephens; worked with Ben Lexcen on *Australia*; *France III*; *Magic*; *Liberty*; *Eagle*

Valicelli, Andrea Italy
IOR yachts; *Brava, Gemini*; *Filo da Torcere*; *Azzurra*

Wallis, Stephen England
Codesigner of *K-25*

Watson, George Lennox Scotland
Designer of most famed English and luxury cruisers in Victorian times; *Britannia* and a host of others

Stephens

Wallis

Watson

WINNERS AND LOSERS OF THE AMERICA'S CUP

WINNERS

Year	Boat	Owner/Syndicate	Designer
1851	AMERICA	John C. Stevens Synd.	George Steers
1870	MAGIC	Franklin Osgood	R. S. Loper
1871	COLUMBIA	Franklin Osgood	John Van Deusen
1871	SAPPHO	Wm. P. Douglass	David Kerby
1876	MADELEINE	John S. Dickerson	G. A. Smith
1881	MISCHIEF	Joseph R. Busk	A. Cary Smith
1885	PURITAN	J. Malcolm Forbes Synd.	Edward Burgess
1886	MAYFLOWER	Gen. Charles J. Paine	Edward Burgess
1887	VOLUNTEER	Gen. Charles J. Paine	Edward Burgess
1893	VIGILANT	C. Oliver Iselin Synd.	Nat Herreshoff
1895	DEFENDER	C. Oliver Iselin Synd.	Nat Herreshoff
1899	COLUMBIA	J. P. Morgan Synd.	Nat Herreshoff
1901	COLUMBIA	J. P. Morgan Synd.	Nat Herreshoff
1903	RELIANCE	C. Oliver Iselin Synd.	Nat Herreshoff
1920	RESOLOUTE	Henry Walters Synd.	Nat Herreshoff
1930	ENTERPRISE	Winthrop Aldrich Synd.	Starling Burgess
1934	RAINBOW	Harold S. Vanderbilt Synd.	Starling Burgess
1937	RANGER	Harold S. Vanderbilt Synd.	Starling Burgess / Olin Stephens
1958	COLUMBIA	Henry Sears Synd.	Olin Stephens
1962	WEATHERLY	Henry D. Merce	Phil Rhodes
1964	CONSTELLATION	W. S. Gubelman & E. Ritter Synd.	Olin Stephens
1967	INTREPID	W. J. Strawbridge Synd.	Olin Stephens
1970	INTREPID	W. J. Strawbridge Synd.	Olin Stephens / Britton Chance
1974	COURAGEOUS	R. McCullough Synd.	Olin Stephens
1977	COURAGEOUS	King's Point Fund Inc. Synd.	Olin Stephens
1980	FREEDOM	Fort Schuyler Foundation Inc.	Olin Stephens
1983	AUSTRALIA II	Alan Bond	Ben Lexcen
1987	STARS & STRIPES	Sail America Foundation for International Understanding	Britton Chance / David Pedrick / Bruce Nelson

LOSERS

Year	Boat	Owner/Syndicate	Designer
1851	Fleet of 15	British Yachts	Various
1870	CAMBRIA	James Ashbury	Michael Ratsey
1871	LIVONIA	James Ashbury	Michael Ratsey
1876	COUNTESS OF DUFFERIN	Charles Gifford Synd.	Alexander Cuthbert
1881	ATALANTA	Alexander Cuthbert	Alexander Cuthbert
1885	GENESTA	Sir Richard Sutton	J. Beavor-Webb
1886	GALATEA	Lt. William Henn	J. Beavor-Webb
1887	THISTLE	James Bell Synd.	George Watson
1893	VALKYRIE II	Earl of Dunraven	George Watson
1895	VALKYRIE III	Earl of Dunraven	George Watson
1899	SHAMROCK I	Sir Thomas Lipton	William Fife, Jr.
1901	SHAMROCK II	Sir Thomas Lipton	George Watson
1903	SHAMROCK III	Sir Thomas Lipton	William Fife, Jr.
1920	SHAMROCK IV	Sir Thomas Lipton	Charles E. Nicholson
1930	SHAMROCK V	Sir Thomas Lipton	Charles E. Nicholson
1934	ENDEAVOUR	T. O. M. Sopwith	Charles E. Nicholson
1937	ENDEAVOUR II	T. O. M. Sopwith	Charles E. Nicholson
1958	SCEPTRE	Hugh L. Goodson	David Boyd
1962	GRETEL	Frank Packer Synd.	Alan Payne
1964	SOVEREIGN	James A. J. Boyden	David Boyd
1967	DAME PATTIE	Emil Christensen	Warwick Hood
1970	GRETEL II	Frank Packer Synd.	Alan Payne
1974	SOUTHERN CROSS	Alan Bond	Bob Miller
1977	AUSTRALIA	Alan Bond	Ben Lexcen / Johan Valentijn
1980	AUSTRALIA	Alan Bond	Ben Lexcen / Johan Valentijn
1983	LIBERTY	Fort Schuyler Foundation Inc.	Johan Valentijn
1987	KOOKABURRA III	Taskforce '87 Ltd.	Iain Murray / John Swarbrick

THE 12M RULE

THE RULE

$$\frac{L + 2d - F + \sqrt{S}}{2.37} = 12M$$

This is the formula originated in 1906:

L = The length of the hull measured from a point equal to 1.8 meters above the waterline. Corrections for girth are applied to this measurement.

d = The difference in meters between two measurements around the girth of the hull.

F = Freeboard, the height of the deck above the waterline.

S = The square root of the sail area, including the mainsail and the area of triangle bounded by the mast, forestay, and deck.

2.37 is the mathematical constant.

When all measurements are taken and divided by the constant, the product should be close to 12 meters, or 39.37 feet. This is somewhat confusing for the lay reader, for it implies that the result should be the length of the yacht. Twelve-meter yachts measure between 65 feet and 70 feet in length, have masts that rise 85 feet above the deck, and displace some 25 tons.

The 12M Rule runs to more than 20 pages of finely printed text. The designer is constricted by the formula and must juggle the various measurements to produce the ideal 12-meter yacht, increasing or decreasing the length of the hull, the sail area, or freeboard, and trying to balance all of this with a keel that gives the greatest stability and lateral resistance while causing the least possible forward resistance and which, ideally, actually helps to improve the natural hull speed of the craft. For example, a longer than normal twelve, like the British "Hippo," may have a higher natural hull speed because of her increased length, but the penalty would come in the form of a reduced sail plan. The theoretical gain in speed might not transpire to be a practical gain by comparison with shorter hulls with taller rigs.

The designer must take account of the conditions under which the yacht is likely to be raced; a thorough study of local meteorological conditions, wind speed, and sea state will give an early key as to how the design features could be approached. The breed of 12 meter used off Newport was a very different animal from those used on Gage Roads in the Indian Ocean. When and if the next match is raced off the California coast, designs will change yet again.

PHOTO CREDITS

INDEX